A Manager's Complete Guide to Financial Techniques

A Manager's Complete Guide to Financial Techniques

GEORGE A. ARAGON

THE FREE PRESS
A Division of Macmillan Publishing Co., Inc.
NEW YORK

Collier Macmillan Publishers
LONDON

The Free Press
A Division of Macmillan Publishing Co., Inc.
866 Third Avenue, New York, N.Y. 10022

Collier Macmillan Canada, Inc.

Library of Congress Catalog Card Number: 81–68798

Printed in the United States of America

printing number

1 2 3 4 5 6 7 8 9 10

Library of Congress Cataloging in Publication Data

Aragon, George A.
    A manager's complete guide to financial techniques.

    Includes index.
    1. Corporations—Finance—Handbooks, manuals, etc.
I. Title.
HG4027.3.A7   658.1′5   81–68798
ISBN 0–02–900820–4   AACR2

To Rosemary and our children
Margaret and George Oscar

Contents

Preface

You are reading this book because you want to broaden the scope of your management abilities, increase the value of your management contributions to the company, and thus increase your value as a manager. Whether you help manage a corporation, a partnership, or a proprietorship, the basic techniques presented here will help you achieve these goals. Whether you are the chief executive officer responsible for the "whole show," a division manager responsible for your own part of the show, or a line manager responsible for a particular functional area, the techniques and framework for decisions presented in this book will help make you a more valued manager.

A Framework for Decisions

The financial techniques described in this book all have a common goal: to maximize the *profits* generated from the company's overall *investment* while safeguarding the continuity of operations. This goal can be summarized into a simple relationship known as Return on Investment (ROI):

$$ROI = \frac{profits}{investment}$$

Each of the financial techniques covered in this book has a direct impact on ROI.

This book is not intended to make you an expert in financial techniques. Instead, my objective is to provide an accurate but nontechnical guide to financial techniques. I will describe the purpose of each technique, its assumptions, its major strengths and limitations, and how to apply it. I have tried to keep the presentation "simple but not simple-minded."

Organization of the Book

This book is organized into six major parts:

Part I: The Objectives, Environment, and Fundamentals of Finance
Part II: Ratio Analysis
Part III: Profit Management
Part IV: Working Asset Management
Part V: Capital Budgeting
Part VI: Managing the Cost of Funds

Parts I and II are primarily intended to provide background for the techniques described later. The most important point in these chapters is that ROI should be the primary corporate financial objective, qualified only by the concern for corporate safety.

Part III presents techniques for profit planning and profit management. Part IV discusses methods for improving the management of working capital asset investment. Part V presents methods for maximizing ROI in long-term investment decisions. Finally, Part VI presents methods for minimizing the average cost of funds.

Each part begins with an introduction, which presents the main ideas of that part and provides an overview of the chapters contained.

Each chapter begins with an "Executive Summary," which distills the basic points in the chapter, including a listing of the uses, strengths, and limitations of the techniques covered.

I am grateful for the many helpful comments of Robert O. Aders,

President, Food Marketing Institute; Manuel Aragon, Jr., President, Management Consultants; Professor Jerry Viscione, Boston College; Karen Hanson, financial consultant; William J. Brett, general manager, Barclay Chemical; Anita De Santo, divisional manager, CBS Publications; Robert Aragon, President, Schaefer Bros.; James Chalmers, D.M.D.; Tina Johnson, budget director, Aspen Skiing Corporation; Norman Chambers, project manager, Sub-Sea International; and Mary Sullivan. I also wish to thank Dean John Neuhauser, School of Management, Boston College, and Robert Wallace, The Free Press, for their support and encouragement; and Robert Harrington, The Free Press, for his substantial editorial contributions.

A Manager's Complete Guide to Financial Techniques

## PART ONE

The Objectives, Environment, and Fundamentals of Finance

This part contains the following chapters:

This part discusses why return on investment (ROI) is the most important (though not the exclusive) financial objective and provides the necessary background for the explanation of financial techniques to follow. The role of ROI is examined at three levels:

- as the mechanism in our economy for efficiently allocating capital
- as the most fundamental financial objective of any business
- as an effective management tool for focusing countless business

decisions and activities toward an objective of strategic importance

In order to apply the ROI idea through the use of financial techniques, you must have a basic understanding of financial relationships. Chapter 1 presents the finance viewpoint. Chapter 2 presents the fundamental ROI idea. Chapter 3 describes the organization of the corporation. Chapter 4 discusses the influence of tax factors on corporate financial decisions. Chapter 5 presents the basics of financial statements. Chapters 6 and 7 discuss two principles of financial accounting that can have important impacts on the company's financial statements. These deal with methods of accounting for depreciation and inventory values. You should be aware of their impacts on the financial statements in order better to understand differences among companies or between years for the same company if it has changed its accounting treatments of these items.

The Finance Viewpoint

EXECUTIVE SUMMARY

• The basic idea is that all operating activities of the company have financial implications. These must be tied together into the ROI framework if the company's productivity per dollar of investment is to be maximized.

For every operating action there is a
financial *reaction!*

• The finance perspective is criticized for being overly preoccupied with numbers relative to competitive intangibles. Finance is good at laying everybody's assumptions and estimates out on the table where they can be discussed and evaluated.

Finance is best at telling you:
If THIS then THAT!

At least one top finance officer has suggested that there ought to be more "nonfinance for the finance manager," and I cannot agree more. Just as the nonfinance manager needs to have a working understanding of financial concerns, the *finance* manager must also have a working understanding of the other primary functions of the business.

Functional areas within company management are increasingly intertwined, and these interrelationships are becoming more explicit all the time. There are few business decisions of major importance that don't have important impacts on all functional areas of the company. Nowhere is this clearer than from the standpoint of financial management. I'll say it over and over again, because this is how you begin to think in finance terms:

> For every operating action there is
> a financial *reaction*.

Here are some examples of what I mean:

Example 1. Extending credit to customers may be viewed as a crucial competitive weapon by the sales force. To the finance manager it means possibly greater sales and profits but also fewer cash sales and an immediate reduction in cash inflows. This reduction may have to be made up through increased borrowing from banks. Furthermore, if the change in credit policy is permanent, the finance manager will have to make permanent arrangements for the financing of the increased receivables.

Whether borrowed or financed some other way, whether temporary or permanent, these arrangements will involve financial cost to the company.

Example 2. Cost reduction investments may be considered self-justified by the plant superintendent. To the finance manager, such investments mean greater profits but also additional investment of funds —possibly to the exclusion of other profitable investment opportunities in other parts of the company—or even outside it!

As you will see, it is not enough that an investment increase expected profit for the company. It is necessary that the expected profit *per dollar of investment* is high enough to justify the investment.

Example 3. A closely held company believes it can grow at 30 percent per year given its market potential. In principle, the owner-managers are enthusiastic at the prospect. But will they be willing to do so if the rapid growth rate will require selling stock to outsiders or undertaking levels of debt that could be hazardous? Perhaps they will. But this is a decision that should be made in recognition of the financial implications for the firm.

In summary, operating decisions have financial consequences. The role of the finance manager is to trace through, and where possible anticipate, these consequences.

A Closed System?

If all this begins to sound like the description of a closed system, that is because in many ways, to the finance manager, it is. Financial information comes from the accounting system. The accounting system records every business event—from refilling the employees' coffee pot to replacing the company computer. In the accounting system, there are no "loose ends." Everything is supposed to be counterbalanced to show "for every debit, a credit." This is the heart of the double-entry system of bookkeeping, and this framework carries over into finance. For every business action there is a resulting financial reaction.

Limitations of the Financial Approach

Nonfinance managers sometimes feel improperly second guessed by the "finance guys." In particular, nonfinance managers may object to the emphasis on "numbers" in financial analysis with perhaps little if any direct consideration of strategic intangibles. The finance manager *is* primarily concerned with the dollars-and-cents implications of business performance and decisions, because he is responsible for reporting the "dollars and cents" performance to the company's owners and creditors.

A related concern is that the quantitative approach of financial analysis suggests accuracy or certainty, which may be very misleading. Most—not all, but most—of the techniques used in finance are static types of analysis. In other words, financial analysis doesn't handle uncertainty in a dynamic sense very well. Take a long-term investment decision, for example.

The use of financial analysis in long-term investment decisions involves estimates of results that may extend far into the future; it involves anticipating what the economic life of the investment is and whether any salvage value will be received. Estimates will be needed with respect to market size, market share, price/cost structure, and so on for each year. Economic life of the investment depends to a large extent on the product market as well as a host of technological uncertainties. Salvage value will likewise depend on the economic life of the investment. Attempts to project such factors for ten, fifteen, or even twenty years into the future must be treated skeptically, regardless of their quantitative form. *Today,* even five years is considered "way out." In other words, there is an ocean of uncertainty in the estimates and assumptions employed in financial analyses.

Finance managers generally recognize these limitations. But they will respond that using numerical analysis should be an important part of the decision-making process. They might say: "Nothing handles 'dynamical uncertainty' very well. The answer is not to ignore the figures, just use them carefully."

Finance is very good at telling you,
"If THIS, then THAT."

The "this" part of the equation is not typically the finance manager's responsibility. He gets that from marketing or production projections. If the projections given to the financial analyst are reliable, the analysis itself is likely to be reliable. If the basic information is of dubious quality, the analysis will be of dubious quality.

Because it is quite good at telling you the financial consequences of a given set of numbers, estimates, and assumptions, the financial approach is better than making decisions blind or "by the seat of the pants." These other approaches, after all, will also be based on subjective estimates and assumptions and possibly will also involve extended investment time horizons. The financial approach will put these estimates out into the open, where they can be examined and possibly revised. The key is to know how much weight to put on the financial data. But that is an exercise in managerial judgment.

The Language of Business

Finance terminology is inescapable in business. Words like "profits," "assets," "cash flow," "budgets," "shareholders," "leverage," "ROI," and so on enter daily discussions across all functional areas. As one chief executive of a multinational company pointed out to me, "knowing financial terms and techniques is as important to my effectiveness as knowing the language of the country I happen to be doing business in. You can miss a lot in the translation!''

A Basic Performance Standard

Regardless of your position in the business hierarchy, some form of financial standard is probably being applied to your performance. For a chief executive officer, that standard may be the return on owners' investment; for a division manager, it may be return on corporate investments under your control; for a line manager, it may be an operating budget.

Increasingly managers are finding that they must compete aggressively for a share of corporate resources. Whether in the form of operating or capital budgets, the basis for allocating available funds among managers is the productive use of those resources. Managers who demonstrate that they can do more with what they have will get more.

Finally, regardless of the company's organizational form, as you move up the corporate ladder and assume broader and broader responsibilities, you will find that performance standards will converge on the ROI idea, because, in effect, the ROI idea encompasses performance of all functional areas.

The techniques presented in this book are intended to help you understand the role of finance in maximizing profit and value for your company and to increase your value as a manager.

## 2

The ROI Idea

EXECUTIVE SUMMARY

ROI is more important than profits alone, because ROI measures the profit-making efficiency of a firm. For a given level of investment, you will earn more profits from a high-ROI company than a low-ROI company.

Companies with high ROIs attract investors: Money flows to them. The values of these companies increase, and opportunities for growth can be exploited. Companies with low ROIs are avoided by investors. The values of these companies decrease, and they become less competitive.

The ROI concept is not only important to the company, it is fundamental to the capital allocation process in our economy.

From the standpoint of the company, ROI has implications for

- research and development
- expansion

- technological innovation
- aggressive marketing
- managerial quality
- competitive pricing
- ability to withstand adverse conditions

Many firms have adopted the divisional form of organization in order to improve overall ROI by evaluating the ROI performances of individual division managers. This allows the top management of the company to identify the contributors to performance and the problem areas.

However, even when companies are organized on other control bases and employ other performance measures, such as budgets, costs, revenues, or profits, each contributes to the overall ROI of the company.

The General Idea

ROI stands for *R*eturn *O*n *I*nvestment, and it measures the profits generated by a business relative to the amount of investment required to produce those profits. It is, therefore, a ratio:

$$\text{ROI} = \frac{\text{profits}}{\text{investment}}$$

In an important sense, ROI measures the productivity of business investment because it indicates the ability of the business to create new economic value.

As a measure of business productivity, ROI is also an indicator of management performance. High productivity means high management performance; low productivity means low management performance.

Assume that you manage company A and a rival manages company B. Each of you has the same amount of investment in the business but you have a much higher ROI:

	A	B
ROI	20%	10%

Your ROI is twice as high as that for manager B. In other words, you produce twice as much profit as manager B for the same level of investment.

Your 20 percent ROI means that you produce profits equal to 20 percent of the amount of investment under your management. Your rival is producing profits equal to only 10 percent of the amount of investment under his management. If you each manage $1,000,000 of investment.

Company A profits = .20 X $1,000,000 = $200,000
Company B profits = .10 X $1,000,000 = $100,000

Why Investors Are Interested in ROI

Investors are very interested in the ROI of businesses because the ROI productivity tells them what they can expect to earn on their investment.

Let's say an investor has $1,000 to invest. If he invests in your company he will earn 20 percent on his money (this is equal to $200). If he invests in your competitor, company B, he will earn 10 percent on his money ($100).

It is obvious that the investor will prefer your company to company B. Other investors also will avoid company B, and its value as a company will fall (needless to say B's manager will also be viewed as less valuable). Investors currently in company B will wonder why, being in the same line of business, company A is so much more productive.

ROI and the Economy

In the financial/economic system the flow of money is directed by the promise of the greatest return on investment for a given level of risk. The companies and industries that are able to generate the highest ROI will be those producing goods and services most desired by consumers.

A sudden demand for bicycles will raise prices and make bicycle companies unusually profitable, yielding greater profits per dollar of investment. A sudden decrease in demand for "gas guzzlers" will result in a decrease in prices and profits realized per dollar of investment in the automotive industry.

Investors will invest in bicycle companies instead of gas guzzler manufacturers. Funds will flow to bicycle companies, allowing them to expand and produce more bicycles. Fewer gas guzzlers will be produced.

By directing the flow of money, the ROI mechanism helps ensure that in the long run the most desired goods and services are produced in the desired amounts and that the least desired goods and services are not produced.

ROI and the Company

A company's ROI has a direct and powerful impact on its value. A company with high ROI relative to competitors will attract investors since they get more for their money with a high-ROI company than a low-ROI one. A company with low-ROI performance will lose investors.

> When a company is attractive to investors,
> its value increases.
> When a company loses attraction to investors,
> its value decreases.

There are other important reasons for a company to be concerned with its ROI. For example, since ROI represents the generation of profits by the company, a company with high ROI is generating more funds for research and development, expansion, technological upgrading, aggressive promotional campaigns, and so on. And a company with a high ROI is in a better price-competitive position and is better able to weather adverse economic conditions. The opposite is true for companies with low ROI. In fact, companies with low ROI are extremely vulnerable to an even further weakening of performance precisely because they cannot finance aggressive marketing and competitive production methods.

ROI Within the Company

The strategic importance of ROI performance to the firm as a whole extends to all parts of the company. Many firms try to control the collective ROI performance of the company by decentralizing operating responsibilities and examining the ROI performance of individual managers. This allows the top management of the company to identify the contributors to performance and to sort out "problem" areas. Evaluation and control on this basis, however, must be done carefully since risk differentials and industry conditions, while they can impor-

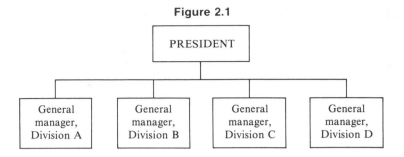

Figure 2.1

tantly affect performance, are beyond the immediate control of the manager.

Figure 2.1 shows what a divisional organization structure is like. In such organizations, the head of each division is usually evaluated on the basis of ROI performance.

The overall ROI of the company will reflect the average ROIs of the divisions. Top management can examine the sources of the overall ROI, rewarding those with high performance and taking corrective action with respect to poor performers.

However, even when the company is organized on some basis other than divisions, each organizational unit contributes in some way to the overall ROI performance of the company. Figure 2.2, for example, shows a company organized along functional lines.

ROI: The Specific Idea

Up to now I have referred to "return on investment" in general terms. However, the word "investment" has many possible interpretations and each of these has an implication for the calculation and interpretation of ROI.

Figure 2.2

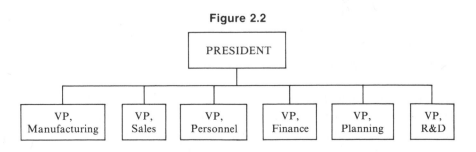

What ROI Means in Practice

"ROI" is liberally defined and used in practice. This is discussed more fully in Chapter 9 ("Profitability"), but right here I would like to alert you to two basic ways in which "ROI" is used:

- Return on Asset Investment (ROA)
- Return on Owners' Investment (ROE)

Return on Assets

Return on assets is measured as the ratio of profits generated to the total assets under the responsibility of management. Thus, return on assets reflects the net impacts of management decisions and actions along with the business environment of the company during a period of time. Since it reflects the efficiency of all assets under the control of management, return on assets is an intuitively understandable measure of performance.

Within the company, return on assets is the most common expression of the ROI idea applied to performance.

Return on Owners' Investment (Return on Equity)

The owners of the company supply the equity invested by the company. Return on equity is measured as the ratio of profits generated to the total investment capital provided by the owners of the company. Thus, return on equity measures the profitability with which the owners' money was managed. Since executive management is directly answerable to the owners, maximizing return on equity within tolerable limits of risk is a vital and proper concern of executive management.

At the top level of executive management and outside the company, Return on Equity is the most common expression of the ROI idea applied to company performance.

Why I Prefer to Focus on Return on Assets in this Book

In view of the preceding discussion it may surprise the reader that I prefer to use return on assets as a focus of performance measurement. There are really two good reasons for this.

Figure 2.3   Two Ways of Looking at ROI

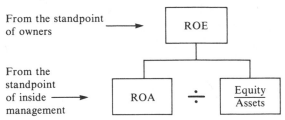

Maximizing ROA Means Maximizing ROE.   Return on owners' equity is directly related to the company's return on assets. As you can see from Figure 2.3, ROE is jointly determined by a company's ROA and its ratio of owners' equity to total assets. (NB: this is explained more fully later; just try to get a general feel for the relationships right now.) This relationship is more explicitly described in Table 2.1. Figure 2.4 shows what happens to ROE as ROA increases, given a fixed ratio of owners' equity to total assets.

Return on Assets Is More Focused on Operating Decisions and Performance.   Since return on equity combines operating performance with the financing decisions made by executive management, it is less precise in identifying opportunities for improving operating performance. Moreover, within the company operating management cannot relate meaningfully to the idea or measurement of owners' equity. For example, a division manager will have a much better sense of the value

TABLE 2.1.   Relationship of Return on Assets (ROA) and Return on Equity (ROE) (Assuming Constant Ratio of Equity to Assets)

Assumed Ratio of Equity to Assets	If ROA Is	ROE Will Be
.5	5%	10%
.5	10%	20%
.5	15%	30%
.5	20%	40%
.5	25%	50%
.5	30%	60%
.5	35%	70%
.5	40%	80%

Figure 2.4 Relationship of Return on Asset (ROA) and Return on Equity (ROE) Assuming Constant 50 Percent Ratio of Equity to Assets

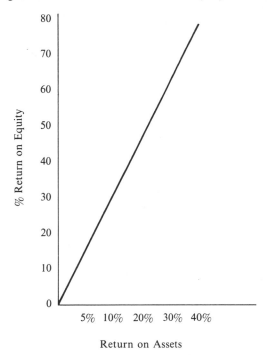

Return on Assets

of assets under his control than of the level of equity represented by those assets.

Therefore, when I say "return on investment" I am referring to "return on assets."

Investment Management Means Asset Management

The general manager of a retail company said to me once: "I was comparing the performance of our retail store located in the South with the one we have in the West. I was concerned because the ROI for the Western store was over 40 percent while that for the Southern store was slightly over 20 percent. What particularly bothered me was that I knew the Southern manager was an aggressive cost cutter and a smart buyer. When I looked at profits relative to sales, sure enough, the Southern manager was squeezing out a lot more profit per dollar of sales than the Western manager. Then it became clear, the Southern manager was buying in larger quantities from suppliers. That allowed him lower product costs than the Western manager, but his inventory level was enormous. In other words, what the Southern manager was saving on product costs he was more than losing by the much larger investment base he was tying up. I pointed this out to him. The following year he outperformed the Western manager.''

The Southern manager was simply not managing his investment base as aggressively as his costs.

For a given level of investment, maximizing profits is the same thing as maximizing ROI. However, it is critical to recognize that the level of investment is not a "given." In other words, the level of investment required to produce profits must be managed effectively.

As a practical matter, the money that investors put into the company is used to acquire operating assets. In effect, the manager manages assets rather than investment itself.

The need to manage assets as agressively as profits is, quite possibly, the least appreciated financial idea. It is so little appreciated, in fact, that the bulk of this or any other standard finance textbook is more directly concerned with the management of assets than with the management of profits!

ROI Comparisons

In making ROI comparisons between companies or between managers it is important to recognize several factors beyond the control of the firm or manager. First, ROI performance is related to the level of risk assumed in the company or in the division. One company may have higher ROI simply because it has assumed higher risk, and vice versa. Second, companies may change certain accounting practices from one period to the next, producing an ROI performance that is not directly comparable even from one year to the next. Companies differ in their accounting practices, and this too can undermine comparability. Third, to an important extent ROI data can be manipulated in a great variety of ways to "boost" performance. Indeed, there are many ways in which this can be done without violating generally accepted accounting principles.

Fourth, the industry in which a firm or company operates has great influence over the performance of the firms within the industry. When comparing companies or divisions in different industries, it is

Figure 2.5 Annual Rates of Profit on Stockholders' Equity After Taxes, Selected Industries, 1980

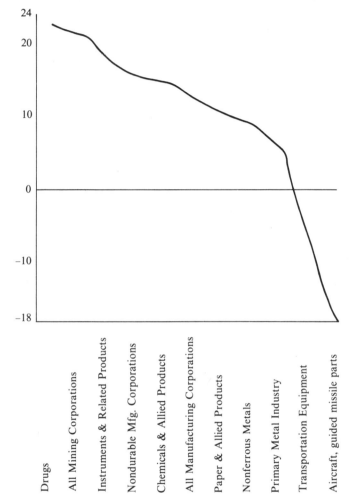

SOURCE: Division of Financial Statistics, Federal Trade Commission, *Quarterly Financial Report for Manufacturing Corporations.*

necessary to keep the overall industry performance in mind: Even "good" managers will experience poor ROI if the industry is depressed, and "poor" managers may look good if the industry is doing very well.

Figure 2.5 shows the broad range of returns on shareholders' equity earned by selected industries during 1980.

Fifth, there may be regional economic differences. If one

manager, say the Western manager, is in an expanding region while, say, the Northeast manager is in a contracting region, the Western manager will look good and the Northeast manager will look bad.

Finally, consideration must be given to the amount of freedom division managers are permitted. A division manager should not be evaluated on operating performance over which he does not possess effective control. In other words, it would not be appropriate to evaluate a plant manager on the basis of ROI if he has control over costs but not sales or the asset investments. Such a manager, however, is helping to determine overall ROI, and he should be evaluated on the basis of that contribution.

3

Corporate Organization

EXECUTIVE SUMMARY

The common stockholders are the owners of the corporation. Preferred stockholders do not own or control the corporation, but they are entitled to specified dividends before the common stockholders.

Creditors lend money to the company. By convention, short-term creditors are those who require payment in one year or less. Most short-term credit must be paid in less than sixty days. Long-term creditors are willing to wait more than a year for payment.

Legally, common stockholders delegate most decisions to the board of directors. The board of directors, in turn, while setting basic corporate policies, delegates authority for most operating decisions to the company's chief executive officer. In practice, the company's executive management exercises almost complete control of the company.

The form of business organization, whether proprietorship, partnership, or corporation, is determined by a wide range of complex legal, personal, tax, and other considerations. This book will focus on the corporation, primarily because of the overwhelming economic significance of this type of business organization. Still, the techniques and principle described in this book are directly relevant to all types of business organizations, including proprietorships and partnerships.

Incorporation

Perhaps the distinctive feature of the corporation is that it has separate legal standing. In the eyes of the law, the corporation is a "person" with distinctive rights and responsibilities apart from its owners. Thus, the affairs of the corporation (including its operations and obligations) cannot be commingled with those of its owners beyond their direct investment in the corporation. This is quite different from proprietorships and general partnerships, in which the activities of the business are viewed as extensions of the owners.

Investors

There are three broad groups of investors in the company:

- Creditors supply short-term and long-term debt to the company
- Preferred shareholders get dividends before common shareholders
- Common shareholders own the company

A company's *financial structure* is made up of all "funds" supplied to the company. A company's *capital structure* is made up of long-term (that is, invested for more than one year) funds. A company's *liabilities* represent "funds" that will have to be repaid.

Creditors

Creditors are those who extend credit to the company. Short-term creditors expect to be paid in twelve months or less. Short-term credit includes things like accounts payable, bank loans and accrued obligations. Accounts payable, a major source of short-term financing, usually must be paid in thirty to forty-five days. Long-term credit is extended for more than a year and includes such things as mortgages and bonds.

Preferred Shareholders

Although preferred shareholders have preferred status relative to common shareholders, preferred shareholders do not own the company. They usually are not entitled to vote in the affairs of the company, and they are limited as to the dividends they can receive. Preferred stock has fallen from favor as a source of financing, and most companies have little if any preferred stock outstanding. When preferred stock is issued (sold) by the company, investors receive a promised, stipulated dividend at regular intervals (e.g. quarterly). The company is not required to pay the promised dividends, but no dividends can be paid to common stockholders until all promised dividends are paid to preferred shareholders.

If the company should be forced into bankruptcy, the preferred shareholders get their investment out after creditors but before the common shareholders do.

While preferred stockholders are exposed to considerably less risk than the common shareholders are, the common shareholders stand to gain much more than preferred shareholders if the company is profitable.

Common Shareholders

Although the corporation has a separate legal standing, it is the creation of its owners. The corporation's owners are those investors who provide *equity* funds to the company. Like all other investors, common stockholders expect to earn a return on their investment. However, the return common stockholders expect is highly uncertain. Because of this risk, common stockholders expect, in the long run, to earn more on their investments than do other types of investors. Sometimes these expectations are realized, sometimes they are not.

To certify their ownership, stockholders receive shares of common stock. The common stock certificates entitle the holders to receive all the net income earned by the business (*after* the dividends due to preferred shareholders, as discussed above) and any liquidation value of the business after all senior claims have been paid.

In large companies shareholders defer most voting decisions to others more knowledgeable and up to date in the affairs of business and financial markets. Shareholders do this by delegating major business decisions to a *board of directors,* which they elect.

In principle the board of directors sets the major policies and goals of the company but in turn delegates day-to-day operating decisions and authority to executive management, headed by the chief executive officer and his vice-presidents. In practice, executive management plays a crucial role in both shaping and implementing corporate policies.

Financial Policies

A company's financial policies fall into three broad areas:

- Investment policy
- Debt policy
- Dividend policy

Investment Policy.   Investment policy relates to the kinds of assets to be acquired; the minimal ROI and other criteria required for consideration; and the procedure by which they will be evaluated.

Debt Policy.   Debt policy is an extremely difficult concern because it determines the amount of debt relative to owners' investment that the company will use. Generally, the more debt the company uses, the higher the return on equity will be. However, more debt means more risk.

High use of debt raises the possibility that the company will go bankrupt if business conditions sour. Short of bankruptcy, excessive debt may severely restrict management flexibility, permitting lenders to intervene in company decisions.

Dividend Policy.   The company operates in order to earn profits. Profits may be either paid out as dividends to stockholders or reinvested in the business. Profits that are reinvested are called "retained earnings." Thus, the retained earnings account represents a continuing account of reinvested profits over the lifetime of the company. Assume that the company shows the following history of profits, dividends, and retained earnings pattern:

Year	1	2	3	4	5
Beginning retained earnings balance	0	20	70	115	175
+ Profits	20	50	75	100	200
− Dividends	0	0	− 30	− 40	− 60
Ending retained earnings balance	20	70	115	175	315

While shareholders could demand all earnings to be paid out as dividends, this is not usually a good idea since the company needs cash for growth. A primary source of such cash is profits reinvested.

A common misunderstanding is that the retained earnings account somehow represents the amount of cash the company has. This is wrong, of course. Retained earnings represents earnings that have been reinvested in the company. In other words, the retained earnings "cash" has been used to buy plant and equipment, build up inventories, support accounts receivable, and so on.

When opportunities for profitable investment are numerous, the company should keep dividends to a minimum and reinvest profits. When profitable growth opportunities become scarcer relative to the profits generated by the business, the company should increase dividends in order to permit shareholders to invest elsewhere.

When a company is reinvesting profits to exploit investment opportunities, the prospect of even larger possible dividends in the future increases the value of company ownership—reflected in an increase in the price of the company's common stock. This rise in stock price is a *capital gain*. Therefore, common stock investors make money both through the dividends they may receive and capital gains they may realize. But notice that *all* of this stock value is ultimately based on the amount, timing, and certainty of future dividends, because that is all the corporation will ever pay out to shareholders.

## 4

The Corporate Tax Environment

EXECUTIVE SUMMARY

Federal taxes heavily influence almost all strategic business decisions, including:

- Form of business organization
- Financing choices
- Investment value and timing
- Use of earnings

The form of business organization is influenced because the *rate* of taxation on profits varies depending on the form of organization. For example, a proprietorship is taxed at the owner's personal tax rate; a corporation has its own tax rate, which may be higher or lower than those of its owners.

Financing choices are influenced because the cost of debt financing is tax deductible while the costs of other types of financing is not.

Tax regulations affect the values of potential investments through the rates at which investments may be depreciated ("written off"). Tax regulations also provide incentives for long-term investment by permitting investment tax credits.

Tax regulations affect the distribution of corporate earnings. The tax rate on dividends is higher than it is for capital gain income. Thus, there are strong incentives for companies to restrict dividends to stockholders and to reinvest earnings.

Tax rates vary with the level of pretax profits generated and with the type of legal organization of the business. However, in order to keep the calculations in this book simple, I will assume in all cases a constant corporate tax rate of 50 percent.

The structure of Federal tax provisions has the effect of directing (if not controlling) business decisions in a number of fundamental respects. Among other things, the tax environment influences

- the form of business organization
- the nature and timing of investments (and divestitures)
- the timing, magnitude, and form of distribution of business profits
- the type of financing employed by the firm

Corporate taxation parallels that for individuals. There are essentially two different tax schedules for corporations: ordinary income and capital gain income. In most cases corporate earnings are subject to the ordinary income tax schedule since earnings are typically generated by the business activities of the firm. At times, however, corporations generate income through a profitable sale of assets. This type of income is taxed as a capital gain.

Corporate Tax Rates

Corporate tax schedules are continually being revised.* The tax schedule on ordinary business income as of 1979 is shown below.

---

* As this book went to press, numerous changes in tax laws were enacted by Congress. The principles discussed in this book are not materially affected.

1979 Corporate Tax Rates

Taxable Income	Tax Rate (%)
1st $25,000	17%
2nd $25,000	20%
3rd $25,000	30%
4th $25,000	40%
over $100,000	46%

To see how this works, assume a corporation earns taxable income of $200,000. The first $25,000 is taxed at 17 percent, for a tax liability of $4,250. The amount between $25,000 and $50,000 (the second $25,000 of taxable income) is taxed at 20 percent, for a tax liability of $5,000, and so on. The table below shows how the overall tax liability and effective tax rate are calculated.

Taxable Income	Tax Rate	Tax
$0–25,000	.17	$4,250
$25,000–50,000	.20	$5,000
$50,000–75,000	.30	$7,500
$75,000–100,000	.40	$10,000
$100,000–$200,000 (total)	.46	$46,000
	Total tax liability	$72,750

Effective tax rate is calculated by dividing the total tax liability by the taxable income:

$$\text{Effective tax rate} = \frac{\$72,750}{\$200,000} = .36$$

In order to simplify the calculations in this book, I shall assume a constant tax rate of 50 percent on ordinary income.

In addition to the ordinary income generated by the company, income may also be realized in the form of capital gains. A capital gain results when the company sells an asset for more than its purchase cost. If the asset has been owned for more than a year, the profit is considered a long-term capital gain. The tax on this type of income is a maximum of 28 percent.

Tax Losses

A corporation that experiences a pretax loss in a given year may be eligible for a tax refund. Under current provisions, a loss in the current year can be consolidated with pretax profits in any of the three previous years (a "carryback") or used to offset future pretax profits in the following seven years (a "carryforward"). Normally, a current year loss will be offset against profits in the earliest of the three previous years.

Ace Company has experienced the following profits and tax liabilities:

	19X1	19X2	19X3	19X4
Profit before taxes	100	120	150	(500)
Tax	50	60	75	(250)
Profit after taxes	50	60	75	(250)

19X4 results reveal a pretax loss of $500. The $500 loss is first consolidated with 19X1 results. 19X1 will use up $100 of the 19X4 loss. Thus, the tax payment of $50 in 19X1 will be refunded. Next, 19X2 pretax profits absorb $120 more of the remaining $400 pretax 19X4 loss. Since the consolidated losses exceed 19X2 pretax income, the tax payment of $60 in 19X2 is refunded. Since losses of $280 in 19X4 are still unabsorbed, they are consolidated with 19X3 results and absorb the $150 pretax profits in 19X3, reducing (on a restated basis) this tax liability in 19X3 to zero. Thus, a further refund of $75 will be received. At the end of 19X4, having losses set against pretax income in the three previous years will result in a consolidated performance over the period 19X1–19X4:

Profit before taxes	(130)
Taxes	(65)
Profit after Taxes	(65)

As of the end of 19X4, total tax credits of $370 have been received. Additionally, losses of $130 after application of all carrybacks are available for use against possible pretax profits in the following seven years, 19X5–19Y1. Assume that 19X5 produces pretax profits of $130. Without a carryforward loss, tax liability in 19X5 would have been $65. However, with the availability of the carryforward loss of $130, consolidated pretax profit in 19X5 becomes zero, resulting in no tax liability. When you total all tax credits and savings resulting from the pretax loss of $500 in 19X5, savings of $250 will be realized. This is the rationale for corporations to show after-tax losses that are less than pretax losses.

The tax treatment of pretax losses also explains why companies that have been unprofitable may still appear to be attractive merger partners: Their losses can be used by the acquiring corporation to reduce tax liability. However, acquisitions solely for the purpose of using tax losses, if proved by the IRS, can disqualify the acquiring company from using the losses acquired.

Tax Payment Schedules

Generally corporations are required to estimate total tax liability for the current year. The corporation is required to pay approximately one-fourth of the total estimated liability on a quarterly basis. Companies whose fiscal year ends December 31 must make payments for anticipated tax liabilities on the fifteenth day of April, June, September, and December. Since there is an obvious temptation to underestimate tax liability, the IRS assesses a penalty if the corporation's estimated tax liability turns out to be less than 80 percent of the actual liability.

Investment Tax Credit

As an inducement to long-term capital investment, tax laws permit a tax credit (or refund) to be taken for new long-term fixed investment. The investment tax credit has the effect of reducing the cost of the investment to the firm and thus should encourage greater investment. The increased investment in turn promotes jobs and national income (and greater tax revenues). The size of the tax credit influences investment: The greater the credit, generally, the greater the incentive for investment. Thus the investment tax credit is raised during periods of economic stagnation and lowered during high economic activity.

Tax Impact upon Financing Choice

Current tax laws favor the use of debt financing. Specifically, the after-tax cost of debt is less than its pretax cost, because interest payments on debt are tax deductible. For example, assuming a 50 percent tax bracket, the effective cost of debt financing is about half its stated rate. Consider the following example with debt and without debt:

A company has debt which has interest payments of $8 per year. Its after-tax cost is only $4. Assume it had pretax earnings of $100 and interest payments of $8.

	With Debt	Without Debt
Earnings before interest and taxes (EBIT)	100	100
Interest	8	Ø
Earnings before taxes (EBT)	92	100
Tax (50%)	46	50
Net income (NI)	46	50

Notice that after-tax earnings without any debt payments equal $50. With $8 of debt payments, after-tax earnings drop to $46—only $4 below the no-debt level. Thus the effective ("true") cost of debt is only half of its stated amount.

Depreciation Methods

Tax treatment also influences investment values in important ways, though primarily as it impacts on the expenses of the firm. For example, when a company invests in a piece of machinery, the IRS permits part of the machine to be periodically "written off" or "expensed" as depreciation, even though no cash is actually disbursed for the expense (Of course, the cash was paid out when the machine was originally acquired.) The expense does appear on the income statement and therefore reduces reported earnings and taxes *but not cash.*

If X corporation has all cash transactions (except depreciation) notice how profits (and taxes) decrease through the depreciation while the cash balance does not (see table top of page 30). Profits reported are only $15, but the firm actually produces $25 in cash. Taxes would have been $20 rather than the $15 with depreciation. Without depreciation "expense" cash is only $20, but with the depreciation expense cash is $25. The sole reason for this is the fact that depreciation "shielded" $10 of income, of which the IRS would have gotten $5—*but* depreciation did not actually involve an outflow of cash.

With Depreciation

Income Statement		Bank Account	
Sales	100	Cash sales	+ 100
Expenses (except		Expenses (except	
depreciation)	− 60	depreciation)	− 60
Depreciation	− 10	Taxes	− 15
Profits before			
taxes	30	Cash balance	25
Taxes (50%)	− 15		
Net income	15		

Without Depreciation

Income Statement		Bank Account	
Sales	100	Cash sales	100
Expenses	− 60	Expenses	− 60
		Taxes	− 20
Profits before		Cash balance	20
taxes	40		
Taxes	− 20		
Net income	20		

Tax Statement and Public Financial Report

While it is in the corporation's interest to maximize expenses in order to minimize tax liability, such considerations have the obvious effect of reducing reported profits. On the other hand, management desires to report maximum profits. In order to spare management the dilemma of choosing between lower taxes and higher reported profitability, the IRS permits *tax filings* that emphasize allowable deductions and *financial reports* that minimize deductions to the extent allowed under generally accepted accounting principles. For example, the IRS accepts a tax filing from a corporation that employs higher (accelerated) depreciation, even though the company's financial statement employs lower (straight-line) depreciation.

Ace corporation has acquired a machine for $100,000 with an economic life estimated at ten years. In the first year Ace is eligible to report depreciation of $10,000, but to file a tax statement employing accelerated depreciation expense of $20,000 on the machine.

	Tax Statement	Annual Report
Operating income	70,000	70,000
Depreciation (accelerated)	20,000	(straight-line) 10,000
Profit before taxes	50,000	60,000
Taxes	(25,000)	(30,000)
Net income	25,000	30,000

An obvious consequence of the differential treatment is that reported tax payments ($30,000 in the first year) are higher than the actual tax liability ($25,000). As a result, the company cash account will have $5,000 more than the annual report income statement would indicate. The $5,000 differential is called a "deferred tax liability."

Later in the asset's life, when the accelerated method is producing lower depreciation expense, this relationship will be reversed. The corporation's cash account will be lower than indicated by the annual statement, and the deferred account will be reduced.

	Tax Statement	Annual Report
Operating income	70,000	70,000
6th yr. depreciation	(accelerated) − 3,355	(Straight-line) − 10,000
Profit before taxes	66,645	60,000
Taxes	− 33,323	− 30,000
Net income	33,322	30,000

In actuality if the firm continues to expand and apply accelerated methods to new acquisitions, the corporation may never have to reduce the deferred account, as more deferrals will be generated than will be lost. For this reason some view the deferred tax liability as almost equity—on the assumption that the government will never receive it.

Taxation of Dividends and Capital Gains

When a corporation pays dividends to its stockholders, the recipients must pay taxes on the dividends. Furthermore the tax *rate* on dividends is the same as that paid on ordinary income (e.g. wages and salaries). For many investors this tax on dividends can be large.

However, if the company reinvests profits and does not pay dividends, the value of the company will increase and the price of the company's common stock will increase. If a stockholder sells his stock at the higher price he will realize a capital gain. He will be taxed on this capital gain, but if he has owned the stock for at least a year the tax rate will be much lower than that for dividends. Therefore, stockholders generally prefer a dollar of capital gains to a dollar of dividend income. This has the effect of encouraging companies to reinvest profits rather than to pay dividends. However, most companies do a little of each.

## 5

Basics of Financial Statements

EXECUTIVE SUMMARY

There are three fundamental financial statements prepared:

- Income statement
- Balance sheet
- Funds flow statement

The income statement outlines the operating performance of the company during some period of time. It matches costs of producing sales with the sales generated. Sales minus the costs incurred result in the profits of the business.

The balance sheet identifies the assets owned by the corporation and the manner in which they were financed as of a specific point in time. The balance sheet balances the total purchase price of assets, less depreciation, with the sources of financing currently being used.

The funds flow statement identifies the changes in a balance sheet during a period of time.

Before embarking on an exploration of financial techniques, you need to understand financial statements. This chapter provides the basic building blocks you will need in handling the material that follows.

Income Statement

The bottom line is profits. Profits are generated by *sales* of goods and services, which the company either creates or transfers from other producers to other buyers. Sales involve *expenses,* obviously *cost of goods sold,* but also *operating expenses,* such as *selling, general* and *administrative,* and *depreciation. Nonoperating expenses* include *interest* on borrowing. The *sales/expense/profit* relationships are summarized in the *income statement,* like the one shown in Table 5.1. Note how many types of "profit" there are.

Sales minus cost of goods sold produce gross profit. Gross profit minus operating expenses result in operating profit. (Another popular name for operating profit is earnings before interest and taxes, or

TABLE 5.1. Tasbem Co. Income Statement

For the Year Ending December 31, 19X2		
Sales		$1,000,000
Cost of goods sold		600,000
Gross profit		400,000
Operating expenses:		
Selling	50,000	
Gen'l & admin.	100,000	
Depreciation	50,000	200,000
Operating profit (EBIT)		200,000
Nonoperating expenses:		
Interest		20,000
Earnings before taxes		180,000
Taxes (50%)		90,000
Net income		90,000

EBIT for short. I shall refer to EBIT often). Operating income less nonoperating expenses produce earnings before taxes (or profits before taxes, or income before taxes, or pretax income—these all mean the same thing). Earnings before taxes minus tax liability produce earnings after taxes (or, equivalently, net income). The net income line is *the* bottom line on the income statement.

Cash Flows

It would be misleading to think of the net income as the net amount of *cash flow* generated by the business during the period. For most firms there is little relationship between the flow of income from the business and the flow of cash, since the items that appear on the income statement are not all cash transactions. For example, sales made on credit will show up on the income statement as sales, allright, but no cash will flow into the company's bank account until the credit sales are collected. On the other hand, not all of the expenses shown on the income statement will represent cash outflows during the accounting period. Purchases of raw materials from suppliers on credit may show up as cost of goods sold but won't have any effect on the company's cash balance until the credit purchases are actually paid for.

> A retailer purchased $1,000 worth of goods from a wholesaler on sixty-day credit and sold them the same day for $1,500 on ninety-day terms. At the end of the month, sales and profits are:
>
> | | |
> |---|---|
> | Sales | $1,500 |
> | Cost of Goods Sold | 1,000 |
> | Gross Profit | 500 |
>
> Ignoring the rest of the income statement, profits are $500, but no cash has changed hands between company and supplier or final purchaser.

Balance Sheet

Probably the least understood or appreciated of the basic relationships is the role of *assets*. Assets are the investments made *by* the company. Liabilities and shareholders' equity represent investments made *in* the company by others.

Assets represent the investments needed to generate the sales to produce the profits we are concerned with. In this sense, assets represent the "business engine"; the more efficient it is, the more sales and profits we can get out of it. But in the long run, more sales require bigger engines. If you can't "buy" a bigger engine, you can't generate more sales, and therefore more profits.

When someone says "Let's increase sales by 10 percent," the first question in your mind should be, "Where do we get the engine to generate that product?" Does that sound like the kind of question the plant foreman might ask? But the finance manager's question is more general. He's not only thinking about where you're going to get more machinery and equipment to produce the goods, he's also worried about how much raw materials inventory you'll need to produce the goods; and how much finished goods inventory you'll need in anticipation of greater sales; and how much of an increase in accounts receivable investments you'll need to support the sales made; and how much more cash you'll need to meet operating transactions; and so on. All of these items represent investments the company has to make in order to produce goods for sales, which will ultimately produce profits. These asset requirements and the manner in which they are paid for are summarized in a *balance sheet* such as the one shown in Figure 5.1.

The balance sheet can be a very informative or a very misleading document. It represents a "snapshot" of the corporation's financial condition at a single point in time—for example, the company's fiscal

Figure 5.1

Investments made by the company

Investments in the company by creditors and shareholders

Tasben Co. Balance Sheet

As of December 31, 19 ___

($000)

ASSETS			LIABILITIES & STOCKHOLDERS' EQUITY		
Cash		10	Accounts payable		75
Accounts receivable		140	Bank loan payable		50
Inventory		100	Total current liabilities		125
Total current assets		250	Long-term debt		200
Gross fixed assets	400		Total liabilities		325
Less: Accumulated			Stockholders' equity		
depreciation	−150		Paid-in capital & surplus	75	
Net fixed assets		250	Retained earnings	100	175
Total assets		500	Total liabilities & stockholders' equity		500

year end. If the fiscal year end is representative of the company's business activity during the year, the statement will tend to be representative. If the fiscal year end is unrepresentative, the statement will tend to be misleading. Furthermore, a number of features of the balance sheet can be changed on short notice: A bank loan can be negotiated or eliminated, trade credit can be repaid, cash can be replenished, accounts receivable can be sold for cash, because of this potential for "window dressing," balance sheet data must be treated carefully.

"I know of a company with a $300 million dollar line of credit—and it uses it heavily during the year, but on December 31 (their fiscal year end) they don't show a nickel of it. They pay it off in December and reborrow in January" (statement by a financial analyst).

The basic function of the balance sheet is to identify all those things owned by the corporation (assets) and to show how they are currently being financed (liabilities and equity). Since every asset must be financed ("paid for") and all financing results in an asset (cash, if nothing else) *the total assets for a corporation must be equal to its total of liabilities plus shareholders' equity.*

Short-term asset investments (i.e., cash and assets that will mature or be converted to cash in a year or less) are known as *current assets.* Current assets include *cash, marketable securities, accounts receivable, and inventory. Long-term assets* are investments committed for longer than a year. *Fixed assets* include land, buildings, and equipment. *Gross fixed assets* represent the total original (historical) cost of all fixed assets. *Accumulated depreciation* represents the total amount of fixed assets "written off" since the date of purchase. *Net Fixed Assets* are the remaining (book) value of all fixed assets. *Intangibles* represent assets such as *goodwill* and *patents* which the company has paid for but whose value is intrinsic.

The company must pay for assets, and it does so with a combination of owners' savings *(equity)* and borrowed money *(liabilities). Current liabilities* are those which will mature in a year or less. These obligations primarily include *accounts payable* (trade-credit), *bank debt,* and accruals. *Long-term liabilities* represent debt that will mature in more than a year.

Other long-term liabilities besides long-term debt also appear on the right-hand side of the balance sheet, *deferred income taxes* perhaps being the most common.

Shareholders' equity (or *net worth*) consists of two principal types of investment by owners. *Paid-in capital and surplus* is the amount of money shareholders paid to the company in exchange for *common stock shares* issued by the company. If you own 10 percent of the common stock shares outstanding, you own 10 percent of the company. *Dividends* represent profits paid to stockholders. *Retained earnings* represent profits reinvested by the owners.

Relationship of Income Statement to Balance Sheet

Retained earnings are increased by the profits earned by the company, less dividends paid. Thus, from one year to the next the increase in the retained earnings account on the balance sheet is equal to profits earned during the year minus any dividend paid.

In an important sense, the income statement is simply a detailed description of the change in retained earnings. Say that during the year, net income earned was $100,00. Dividends of $20,000 were paid out. Thus, the increase in retained earnings was $80,000.

Statement of Changes in Financial Position

One of the most fundamental management tasks is deciding which operations or investments to expand, which to reduce, and which to add. These are decisions made constantly, often unconsciously. Even an unintended buildup of inventory while sales are slackening represents a deployment of corporate assets or funds to inventory rather than, say, to advertising or debt reduction. The funds flow statement provides insights into the "funds deployment" decisions made by the company management over a period of time.

Sources and Uses of Funds

A source of funds represents funds that were made available during the period for redeployment: A reduction of accounts receivable, for example, indicates collections over and above new credit extended and therefore funds available for investment elsewhere. A reduction in inventory means you sold more than you produced, and this added funds available. A reduction in plant and equipment may mean that you sold some fixed assets, and that provided funds available to management. A drawdown from the corporate bank account represents an increase of funds in management's "hands."

Similarly, an increase in bank borrowings and borrowings from other sources provides more funds for management. These all represent sources of funds. As you can see from the examples we have gone through, a source of funds is

- Any decrease in an asset account
- Any increase in a liability and equity account

Uses of funds are really just the opposite of sources. If you buy more plant and equipment (fixed assets) the increase in those assets represents a use of funds. Extending more credit than collections means that accounts receivable will increase, which means that you have used funds to support credit sales. An increase in inventory is the same thing, a use of funds for purposes of increasing an investment. On the other side of the balance sheet, a decrease in debt results from payments made. Paying off debt uses funds. Payments of accounts payable or other current liabilities also use up funds and therefore represent a use of funds. A use of funds is

- Any increase in an asset account
- Any decrease in a liability and equity account

Since the sources and uses of funds statement is based on changes in asset, liability, and equity accounts, it is clearly based on balance sheet relationships. In order to prepare a sources and uses of funds statement, all we really need is two balance sheets. The funds flow statement will trace through the changes in balance sheet between the two periods of time. The funds flow statement must show total sources equal to total uses; otherwise the underlying balance sheets do not "balance."

How to Prepare a Sources and Uses Statement

This is a "quick and dirty" summary of the preparation of a sources and uses statement, and it should be recognized that a number of adjustments are intentionally omitted to keep the presentation uncomplicated. My purpose is to suggest how the statements are prepared.

The interested reader will have no difficulty going on to more detailed formats in other books.

Step 1. Get two balance sheets covering the period of interest (e.g. year ends, 19X1 and 19X2).

TABLE 5–2. Comparative Balance Sheets for the Year End, 19X2 and 19X1

	19X2	19X1	Change
Assets			
Cash & mkt. sec	10	6	+4
Accounts rec.	140	116	+24
Inventory	100	80	+20
Gross fixed assets	$400	$350	
-Accum. deprec.	150	100	
Net fixed assets	250	250	0
Total assets	$500	$452	

	19X2	19X1	Change
Liabilities & Shareholders Equity			
Accounts payable	75	60	+15
Bank loans	50	40	+10
Long-term debt	150	190	− 40
Deferred income taxes	50	37	+13
Shareholders' equity	175	125	+50
	$500	$452	

Uses		*Sources*	
Cash & mkt. sec.	4	Accounts payable	15
Accounts rec.	24	Bank loans	10
Inventory	20	Defer. inc. tx	13
Long-term debt	40	Sh. Equity	50
Total	88		88

Step 2. Compare each of the accounts between the two periods. Note whether there was an increase, decrease, or no change in each account (ignore the items "Gross Fixed Assets" and "Depreciation," as these two are netted in the "Net Fixed Assets" line item).

Step 3. Using the decision rules, put each of the changes into either the "Sources" or the "Uses" column.

Step 4. Total each column and make sure they balance.

An example is shown in Table 5.2.

## 6

Depreciation Methods

EXECUTIVE SUMMARY

There are four basic methods of calculating depreciation:

- Straight-line
- Units of production
- Double-declining balance
- Sum-of-the-years-digits (SYD)

The double-declining balance and SYD methods are accelerated methods since they result in larger charge-offs early in the investment's life than later. The straight-line method results in a uniform, constant charge-off each year. The units of production method results in depreciation charge-offs that reflect the actual level of use, and therefore depreciation with this method varies with the level of production.

You should be familiar with four basic methods of calculating depreciation:

- Straight-line
- Units of production
- Double-declining balance
- Sum-of-the-years-digits

Straight-line

The straight-line method is relatively simple. Annual depreciation expense is simply the cost of the asset less its salvage value divided by the number of years the equipment is expected to last (before either wearing out or becoming obsolete). A machine costing $100,000 with a salvage value of $10,000 and a ten-year useful (economic) life will have $9,000 of depreciation per year.

$$\frac{\text{Cost} - \text{Salvage Value}}{\text{Economic Life}}$$

Obviously, (given the cost of the machine), the amount of depreciation depends in part upon estimated economic life and salvage value. For this reason, the IRS has guidelines (Asset Depreciation Range) for estimating these variables for broad groups of assets.

Units of Production Method

If useful life is measured by use (i.e., units of production) rather than time, the depreciation method is similar to straight-line except that a depreciable cost per unit of production is developed and then multiplied by the number of units produced in a particular period. This depreciation method may be more useful in situations where the production (and use of the machine) is not uniform over the life of the machine. A commercial airliner, for example, might be depreciated on the basis of hours of flying time.

A machine costing $100,000 with a salvage value of $10,000 and a production life of 10,000 units will have depreciation of $9 per unit of production. The actual level of depreciation in a given year will depend upon the volume of units sold, but when 10,000 units have been produced the machine will have been completely depreciated (down to salvage value).

$$\frac{\text{Cost} - \text{Salvage value}}{\text{Production life (units)}}$$

Double-Declining Balance Method

Distinct from the other two methods, the double-declining balance (DDB) method and the sum-of-the-years-digits (SYD) (described next) initially allow companies to accelerate their depreciation on investment. The purpose is to allocate the total depreciation on the machine in such a way that more of the total depreciation is shown in the early years, when it has greatest tax shield value to the corporation. Thus, accelerated methods result in higher depreciation (and lower taxes) in the early years and lower depreciation (and higher taxes) in the later years. The value of receiving cash earlier rather than later is discussed in Part V.

Let us now see how the DDB is used. The DDB method calculates depreciation against the net book value of the asset (and not, as in the

TABLE 6.1. Double Declining Balance (DDB)

Year	DDB%	NBV Beginning	Depreciation	NBV End
1	20%	100,000	20,000	80,000
2		80,000	16,000	64,000
3		64,000	12,800	51,200
4		51,200	10,240	40,960
5		40,960	8,192	32,768
6		32,768	6,554	26,214
7		26,214	5,243	20,971
8		20,971	4,194	16,777
9		16,777	3,355	13,422
10		13,422	3,422	10,000

NOTE: The DDB method, is used until the total depreciation is equal to the *depreciable* value (i.e., cost minus salvage value). Alternatively stated, the DDB method is used until NBV of the machine is equal to salvage value.

Assumptions:
  Original cost = $100,000
  Salvage value = $10,000
  Economic life = 10 years

straight-line and unit of production methods, against the cost minus salvage value). The DDB method is a percentage method in that initially the percentage of the total depreciation is calculated uniformly over the economic life of the method. This percentage is then doubled, and the result is applied to the current book value of the asset.

A machine costing $100,000 with a salvage value of $10,000 and an economic life of ten years will have the following percentage applied to net book value (NBV) each period:

$$\frac{1}{\text{Economic life}} \times 2 = (\frac{1}{10}) \times 2 = 20\%/\text{year}$$

Table 6.1 shows the annual depreciation using the DDB method.

Sum-of-the-Years-Digits (SYD) Method

The SYD method is also an accelerated depreciation method. In using the SYD method, depreciation is based upon the difference between cost and salvage value (like the straight-line method). However, the depreciation rate to be used for a given year (N) is equal to the ratio of years of life remaining on the asset to the sum of the years of economic life.

A machine costing $100,000 with a salvage value of $10,000 and an economic life of ten years has the following depreciation schedule:

$$(\text{Cost–Salvage value}) \times (\frac{\text{Years of life remaining}}{\text{Sum of the year digits}})$$

In the first year,

$$\text{Dep}_1 = (\$100,000 - \$10,000) \times (\frac{10}{1+2+3+4+5+6+7+8+9+10})$$

$$\text{Dep}_1 = (\$90,000) \times (\frac{10}{55}) = (\$90,000) \times (.1818)$$

$$\text{Dep}_1 = \$16,362$$

Table 6.2 contains the annual depreciation charges using the SYD method.

Note that both accelerated methods produce greater depreciation than the straight-line method in the early years. Further notice that in later years the straight-line method produces higher depreciation than the accelerated methods. Fortunately for the corporation, the IRS per-

TABLE 6.2. Sum-of-the-Years-Digits Method

	Dep. %	Dep.
10/55	.1818	16,362
9/55	.1636	14,724
8/55	.1455	13,095
7/55	.1273	11,457
6/55	.1091	9,819
5/55	.0909	8,181
4/55	.0727	6,543
3/55	.0545	4,905
2/55	.0364	3,276
1/55	.0181	1,638
		$90,000

Assumptions:
  Original cost = $100,000
  Salvage value = $10,000
  Economic life = 10 years

mits the corporation to switch from the accelerated methods to the straight-line method for purposes of depreciation expense calculation. The relationship among the depreciation methods is shown in Figure 6.1. A numerical comparison of the three methods is contained in Table 6.3.

Figure 6.1 Comparison of Depreciation Methods: Straight-line, Sum-of-the-Years'-Digits, Double-declining Balance

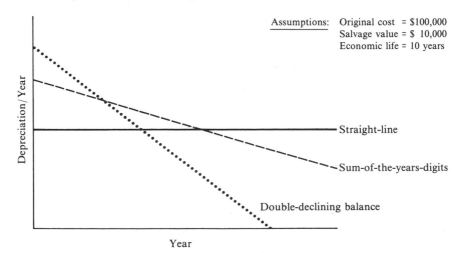

Table 6.3.   Comparison of Depreciation Methods: Straight-line, Units of Production, Double-declining Balance, Sum-of-the-Years-Digits

Year	Straight-line	Units Produced			DDB	SYD
1	9,000	500 × $9	=	4,500	20,000	16,362
2	9,000	500	=	4,500	16,000	14,724
3	9,000	1,000	=	9,000	12,800	13,095
4	9,000	1,000	=	9,000	10,240	11,457
5	9,000	1,500	=	13,500	8,192	9,819
6	9,000	1,500	=	13,500	6,554	8,181
7	9,000	1,500	=	13,500	5,243	6,543
8	9,000	1,000	=	9,000	4,194	4,905
9	9,000	1,000	=	9,000	3,355	3,276
10	9,000	500	=	4,500	3,422	1,638
	$90,000	10,000		$90,000	$90,000	$90,000

Assumptions:
  Original cost = $100,000
  Salvage value = $10,000
  Economic life = 10 Years

Inventory Valuation

EXECUTIVE SUMMARY

During a period of inflation the way you account for inventory can have a big effect on reported performance.

The *first-in-first-out (FIFO)* method will result in higher profits and higher ROI when prices are rising. The method, however, also results in higher taxes.

The *last-in-first-out (LIFO)* method will result in lower profits and ROI than other methods but does reflect more accurately the costs of doing business. The added advantage of the LIFO method is that it minimizes tax liability.

The *average cost* method represents a compromise between the effects of the FIFO and LIFO methods and more uniformly distributes the effect of inflation.

Unfortunately, the IRS does not allow you to use LIFO for tax purposes if you use FIFO for financial reporting.

According to accepted accounting practice a company should value its inventory at the lower of cost or market. In most cases this means valuing inventory at cost.

A problem arises in trying to determine the actual cost of inventory when inventory costs have risen substantially. There is no single, correct method for costing inventory, and a variety of different methods are employed in practice.

The cost assigned to inventory can have a significant impact on the financial statements of the company during a period of accelerating inflation. Therefore, it is important to understand the ways in which inventory costing can affect financial statements.

This chapter discusses three principal methods of inventory costing:

- First-in-first-out (FIFO)
- Last-in-first-out (LIFO)
- Average cost

The Issue

Let's say you purchase frisbees for resale. During the year you receive two shipments of frisbees, 1,000 frisbees in each shipment.

	Shipment # 1	Shipment # 2
Quantity	1,000	1,000
Cost/Unit	$1.00	$1.25

During the year you sell 1,000 frisbees for $1.50 apiece. Now the question is, which frisbees did you sell—the high-cost ones of shipment # 2 or the low-cost ones of shipment # 1. You have a choice, and what you select has an impact on earnings and the balance sheet.

LIFO

According to the LIFO method, you assume that the *most recently* purchased frisbees are the first to be sold. So under the LIFO method, the cost of frisbees sold is $1.25 apiece. The remaining lower-cost frisbees are still in inventory.

Income Statement		Balance Sheet	
Sales	$1500	Cash	—
CGS	1250	A/R	—
Gross profit	250	Inventory $1,000	

FIFO

According to the FIFO method, you assume that the frisbees purchased *earliest* are sold first. So under the FIFO method, the cost of frisbees sold is $1.00 apiece. The remaining higher-cost frisbees are still in inventory.

Income Statement		Balance Sheet	
Sales	$1500	Cash	—
CGS	1000	A/R	—
Gross profit	500	Inventory $1250	

Notice that the FIFO method in this example has the effect of doubling reported gross profit and, ignoring other assets, substantially raises ROI.

	LIFO	FIFO
Gross profit	250	500
Inventory investment	1,000	1,250
ROI	25%	40%

Although FIFO results in "better" reported performance, it has important weaknesses. For example, the "paper profits" result in higher tax liabilities and may raise the dividend expectations of shareholders. These effects reduce the amount of corporate cash at a time when the costs of doing business are increasing. Ultimately, FIFO restricts the company's ability to continue growing.

The LIFO method results in lower reported performance but has certain advantages. For example, it minimizes the adverse tax consequences of inflation and does not unjustifiably raise investors' dividend expectations. Furthermore, the lower-cost inventory shown on the balance sheet represents future profits.

The 1,000 frisbees shown on the balance sheet at a cost of $1.00

apiece now have a market value of $1.50 apiece. When these frisbees are finally sold, the profits will be realized.

Average Cost

An alternative to the biases in the FIFO and LIFO methods is simply to take the average cost of inventory purchases.

Income Statement		Balance Sheet	
Sales	1150	Cash	—
CGS	1125	A/R	—
Gross Profit	375	Inventory	$1125

The average cost method has the effect of distributing the "paper profit" of inflation more uniformly over time.

Why Not Use LIFO for Tax Reporting and FIFO for Financial Reporting?

In choosing depreciation methods, a company has the option of using accelerated depreciation for tax purposes and straight-line for financial statements. Thus, where depreciation is involved, companies minimize taxes and maximize reported performance. The same flexibility is not available for inventory valuation. Under current tax rules you must use LIFO for financial reporting if you use it for tax reports.

## PART TWO

Ratio Analysis

This part contains the following chapters:

The purpose of ratio analysis is to combine pieces of financial information into new information about the financial performance, condition, and potential of the company.

Company A has higher profits and greater investment than Company B. Looking at these items separately, Company A seems to be in "better shape."

	A	B
Profits	$1,000,000	$500,000
Investment	$10,000,000	$2,500,000

But if we combine this information from the financial statements into a ratio, we get a new piece of information which is significant:

	A	B
Profits / Investment	10%	20%

Company B is producing *twice* as much profit on investment as Company A is!

The focus of ratio analysis will vary according to the particular concern of the analyst. Short-term creditors are most concerned with the short-term outlook, because that is the period of their exposure. Long-term investors are more concerned with the long-run viability and profitability of the company.

Profitability ratios provide information about the investment worth of the company. ROI, for example, indicates the ability of the company to generate profits per dollar of investment. However, ROI is an overall measure and sometimes a narrower focus on the profit-*ability* of the company is desired. For example, owners of the company will be interested in the return on owners' investment rather than the return on total investment. Company managers are also interested in knowing the overall productivity of production, purchasing, administrative, and merchandising operations, and this is revealed in the profit margin ratio.

Liquidity ratios provide information about the ability of the company to meet forseeable cash outflows and the amount of "buffer" it has for meeting unexpected cash drains.

Leverage ratios measure the amount of financial risk in the company. The use of leverage can help increase the return on owners' equity substantially. However, excessive leverage can be hazardous to the survival of the company during recessions.

Asset management (efficiency) ratios are very useful in revealing whether—and in what areas—investment management is effective. For example, poor inventory management will result in unnecessarily large inventory investment, which will detract from overall ROI performance. The same is true of poor control of customer credit (accounts receivable).

Market value ratios reveal the assessments by investors about the performance, condition, and prospects of the company.

In order to evaluate ratios, standards are necessary. There are two basic types of standards:

- Industry norms
- Trend analysis

Both of these are used in making judgments about the ratios under consideration.

8

Introduction to Ratio Analysis

EXECUTIVE SUMMARY

This chapter does three things:

- Demonstrates the importance of ratios in financial analysis
- Discusses the major classes of ratios used
- Presents standards for the evaluation of ratios

The purpose of ratio analysis is to help us understand what is really going on in the company on the basis of limited information (usually only the information contained in the financial statements). In addition, ratio analysis alows us to make judgments about the performance and prospects of the company.

If carefully prepared and interpreted, ratio analysis can reveal the "story behind the story," which might otherwise escape inside management itself. For example, from Table 8.1, would you say that the Joy Company is in good shape?

Profits are large, assets are large, and sales are high. These are all "good" things, but actually Joy is on the verge of bankruptcy. The company has excessive debt, most of which will have to be paid soon, and very little cash. In fact, operations may soon cease entirely. One year's ratios could have told you that.

When undertaking ratio analysis, perhaps the most important thing to keep in mind is: "What do I want to know about this company?" Whithout a clear-cut objective, ratio analysis can produce a wilderness of financial information. For example, if our question had been, "How profitable is the company?" we would have focused on the profit performance, possibly even ignoring its serious problems. But the question we did ask was, "Is Joy Company in good shape?" This very different question called for a different, much more general evaluation, which in turn revealed the serious prospect of bankruptcy.

The focus of ratio analysis will vary according to the particular concern of the analyst. Short-term creditors are most concerned with the short-term outlook, because that is the period of their exposure. Long-term investors are more concerned with the long-run viability and profitability of the company. Each of these perspectives will be oriented toward a different set of questions. Even if each of these perspectives were to use the same basic information and methods, they will place different emphasis on the interpretation of the evidence; possibly even reaching different conclusions about the company's condition and performance.

Karen Company has large cash balances and large holdings of marketable securities. Its managers may be pleased with the company's

TABLE 8.1. Joy Company Income Statement for the Year Ending 12/31/X2

Sales	$1,000,000
Cost of goods sold	600,000
Gross profit	400,000
Operating costs	100,000
Earnings before taxes	300,000
Taxes (50%)	150,000
Net income	$150,000

TABLE 8.1 (cont.) Joy Company Balance Sheet, 12/31/X2

Assets		Liabilities and Shareholders' Equity	
Cash	10,000	Accounts payable	300,000
Accounts rec.	190,000	Bank loan	500,000
Inventory	300,000	Current liability	800,000
Current assets	500,000	Long-term debt	300,000
Net fixed assets	1,000,000	Total liability	1,100,000
Total assets	$1,500,000	Stockholders' eq.	400,000
		Total liability and stockholders' eq.	$1,500,000

"liquidity," but shareholders will be unhappy that the funds are not being more profitability invested.

What Are the "Right" Questions?

Whatever the specific question to be answered about the financial condition of a company, it will generally fall into one of the following categories:

- • Profitability
- • Liquidity
- • Market value
- • Efficiency
- • Financial structure

What These Categories Reveal

• Profitability. There are many dimensions to profitability. Each has an impact on the overall profit performance of the company. We may want to examine, for example, the profitability of sales, the profitability of total investment, or the profitability of shareholders' investment, and so on. This is examined in Chapter 9.

• Liquidity tells us how much cash the company can generate on short notice to meet current obligations. It also indicates how much cash the company will be able to generate to undertake needed or desired activities, such as production operations, plant expansion, dividend distribution, and so forth. This will be taken up in Chapter 10.

 • Financial structure. We are interested in financial structure because it tells us how the company's investments have been financed. In particular, this type of analysis reveals the extent to which debt has been used to acquire assets and therefore how much financial risk exists. This is discussed in Chapter 11.

 • Efficiency. Management is most directly concerned with the efficiency of its use of assets. The more efficient the company is in its use of assets, the less funds it will have to raise and the greater its overall profitability will be. This is explored in Chapter 12.

 • Market value ratios reveal how the investment public evaluates the performance and prospects of the company. Since the market value of a company reflects the totality of information about the company, the market value may provide important insights or confirmations of our own evaluation. This is discussed in Chapter 13.

Comparisons

Typically, financial evaluations require comparisons in order to determine whether a company has done well or poorly. In general, there are two types of comparisons that can be used:

 • Trend analysis
 • Industry norms

Trend comparisons look at the performance of a company or division over a period of time. An advantage in this type of comparison is that you are comparing a company on the basis of previous demonstrated performance. A disadvantage is that it ignores factors outside the control of company management, such as economic recession or boom. In other words, a company's performance comparison will be heavily influenced not only by external factors but also by the periods selected for comparison.

	Trend Analysis		
	19X0	*19X1*	*19X2*
ROI	− 10%	+ 20%	+ 10%

For example, ROI has dropped drastically in 19X2 compared to the previous year. But what if 19X1 were a "boom" and 19X2 a "bust"?

Company management might have done an outstanding job to show even a 10 percent ROI.

In evaluating ratios, direction of movement is of prime importance. Positive and negative aberrations will reveal themselves relative to the trend, whether the trend is compared to the company's history alone or compared to industry trend or the trends of major competitors.

In order to get a feel for performance in light of the economic environment, we might compare performance of the company relative to the *norms of the industry* or industries it operates in. Or, more directly, we might compare performance of the company against its chief competitors.

	ROI	
	19X1	*19X2*
Company	20%	10%
Industry norm	20%	2%

An ROI of 10 percent for the company while the industry average was 2 percent would be impressive.

Industrywide comparisons have important disadvantages as well. The main problem is a lack of comparability. For example, comparisons between an industry norm and a multi-industry conglomerate would be almost meaningless. Comparisons between a regional company and the national average might be seriously biased if regional economic circumstances were unusual. Similarly, an industry average may not be meaningful for multinational firms, large firms, small firms, established firms, new firms, and so forth.

Industry Patterns

The kind of business a company is in can have a large influence on its ratios. For example, luxury items with high markups will have much higher profit margins than commodity-type products. Table 8.2 shows selected ratios for assorted industries.

The profit margin on sales for business in tobacco products (wholesale) may be less than 1 percent, for example, while the average for businesses in the retail jewelry industry might range from 3 percent to 6 percent.

TABLE 8.2. Dun & Bradstreet Ratios for Selected Industries

Line of Business (and number of concerns reporting)	Current assets to current debt	Net profits on net sales	Net profits on tangible net worth	Net profits on net working capital	Net sales to tangible net worth	Net sales to net working capital	Collection period	Net sales to inventory	Fixed assets to tangible net worth	Current debt to tangible net worth	Total debt to tangible net worth	Inventory to net working capital	Current debt to inventory	Funded debts to net working capital
	TIMES	PER CENT	PER CENT	PER CENT	TIMES	TIMES	DAYS	TIMES	PER CENT	PER CENT	PER CENT	PER CENT	PER CENT	PER CENT
MANUFACTURING AND CONSTRUCTION														
*2731-32 Books: Publishing, Publishing & Printing (54)	4.21	6.50	13.85	19.68	3.12	4.10	53	6.9	14.1	20.7	37.9	40.6	56.8	7.2
	2.86	**3.92**	**8.22**	**10.60**	**2.04**	**2.86**	**65**	**3.9**	**36.0**	**43.6**	**71.7**	**63.8**	**81.0**	**24.2**
	1.94	1.50	3.70	4.20	1.43	2.00	100	2.9	48.5	67.6	119.8	86.6	173.8	76.3
2831-33-34 Drugs (66)	3.78	8.96	21.30	38.05	3.30	6.68	40	8.4	23.5	22.9	32.8	53.3	64.7	15.4
	2.36	**4.77**	**12.19**	**18.59**	**2.14**	**4.20**	**58**	**6.0**	**38.6**	**31.4**	**56.9**	**67.1**	**96.9**	**34.0**
	1.45	2.26	5.08	8.65	1.74	2.89	89	4.2	62.1	50.7	96.6	134.2	112.1	98.8
3271-72-73-74-75 Concrete, Gypsum & Plaster Products (81)	3.80	4.79	9.68	36.57	2.93	9.12	36	19.7	42.9	12.0	31.2	33.4	68.2	13.1
	2.68	**3.13**	**6.29**	**16.53**	**2.10**	**5.38**	**53**	**10.3**	**60.6**	**29.0**	**61.1**	**56.5**	**141.4**	**42.9**
	1.56	1.42	3.66	8.63	1.53	3.77	74	6.2	80.2	57.1	106.2	84.8	328.6	136.6

WHOLESALING

5045 Confectionery (35)	3.87	1.67	10.76	14.72	16.13	19.32	11	19.2	6.9	38.1	111.1	57.6	57.0	14.5
	2.26	**0.43**	**7.53**	**9.52**	**10.68**	**11.99**	**18**	**12.8**	**13.4**	**70.9**	**158.4**	**98.1**	**84.1**	**33.8**
	1.73	0.25	3.89	4.01	6.39	7.35	27	10.3	30.0	125.4	227.7	129.4	124.8	74.3
5047 Meats & Meat Products (45)	2.67	1.81	21.12	30.13	23.84	35.10	13	100.4	10.2	36.2	78.7	24.2	133.1	19.9
	2.01	**0.86**	**11.58**	**19.05**	**16.01**	**23.45**	**19**	**44.9**	**28.8**	**76.3**	**107.4**	**57.7**	**210.0**	**31.7**
	1.48	0.27	6.63	9.87	9.80	15.15	24	29.9	50.7	116.0	277.4	79.5	329.2	69.2
5098 Lumber & Construction Materials (153)	4.30	2.50	9.82	16.10	7.64	9.28	34	10.5	10.6	23.5	61.0	53.4	46.9	16.0
	2.71	**1.29**	**5.89**	**7.28**	**4.40**	**5.14**	**43**	**6.9**	**22.0**	**51.5**	**109.7**	**80.0**	**95.1**	**28.4**
	1.67	0.44	2.31	2.47	2.77	3.67	58	5.5	39.9	104.5	183.4	107.6	143.9	50.9

RETAILING

5252 Farm Equipment Dealers (92)	2.50	3.07	15.67	19.29	7.06	8.50	17	4.6	7.8	65.0	119.5	96.2	62.6	17.5
	1.67	**1.70**	**8.01**	**8.69**	**4.78**	**5.53**	**30**	**2.9**	**18.1**	**137.3**	**227.4**	**174.5**	**81.3**	**28.6**
	1.35	0.81	2.50	3.46	2.64	3.15	55	2.1	28.7	242.8	374.8	294.2	100.7	60.7
5411 Grocery Stores (137)	2.35	1.71	15.47	48.19	13.51	39.52	**	22.9	38.7	34.2	64.2	85.5	67.9	27.4
	1.66	**0.99**	**10.30**	**23.12**	**9.70**	**21.65**	**	**16.8**	**67.4**	**58.3**	**106.4**	**136.1**	**94.0**	**72.6**
	1.27	0.63	7.28	15.51	6.89	13.00	**	12.8	90.9	84.1	169.5	233.5	124.1	184.0
Discount Stores (224)	2.56	2.86	17.01	23.94	8.80	11.96	**	7.2	12.4	56.8	83.7	101.4	56.5	11.6
	1.87	**1.63**	**11.54**	**15.67**	**6.10**	**7.64**	**	**5.3**	**24.0**	**88.1**	**128.3**	**157.9**	**75.0**	**29.0**
	1.49	0.76	5.87	7.04	4.49	5.28	**	3.9	46.6	130.9	209.3	218.2	94.0	70.3

* Standard Industrial Classification (SIC) categories

Source: Key Business Ratios in 125 Lines (New York: Dun & Bradstreet), 1975. Reprinted by permission of Dun & Bradstreet, a Company of The Dun & Bradstreet Corporation.

Table 8.3. Tasbem Company Balance Sheets as of 12/31 (in thousands of dollars)

	19X2	19X1		19X2	19X1
Cash & mkt. sec.	$10	$6	Accounts payable	$75	$60
Accounts receivable	140	116	Bank loan	50	40
Inventory	100	80	Total current liab.	$125	$100
Total current assets	$250	$202	Long-term debt	150	190
Gross fixed assets	400 350		Deferred income		
-Acc. dep.	150 100		Taxes	50	37
Net fixed assets	250	250	Total liabilities	$325	$327
Total assets	$500	$452	Shareholders' Equity:		
			Paid-in capital	75	75
			Retained earnings	100	50
			Total liabilities & shareholders' equity	$500	$452

Table 8.4.   Tasbem Company Income Statements for the Years Ending 12/31

		19X2		19X1
Sales		$1,000,000		$920,000
Cost of goods sold		600,000		533,600
Gross profit		400,000		386,400
Operating Expenses:				
Selling	$50,000		$47,000	
Gen'l & admin.	100,000		92,000	
Depreciation	50,000	200,000	53,000	192,000
EBIT		200,000		194,400
Interest		20,000		18,900
Earnings before taxes		180,000		175,500
Taxes (50%)		90,000		87,750
Net income		$90,000		$87,750

High-priced items tend to have slower sales than commodity-type goods, so it would not be surprising to find that the inventory turnover on high-margin goods is slower than that for commodity-type goods. Inventory turnover for tobacco wholesaling companies may average about seventeen times, while the inventory turnover for retail jewelry stores may average less than three times.

Businesses that sell "large-ticket" products will have to give customers time to pay and hence are likely to have relatively long average collection periods. Businesses in which extending such credit is unnecessary will have low average collection periods. Grocery stores typically extend little or no credit, thus the average collection period is likely to be close to zero. Retail furniture stores, on the other hand, might average one hundred or even two hundred days for their collection period.

For purposes of the financial analysis to follow, consider the comparative income statements and balance sheets for the Tasbem Company covering the years 19X1 and 19X2 (Tables 8.3 and 8.4).

Chapters 9 through 13 illustrate the calculation and interpretation of the most important financial ratios. These chapters are primarily intended to provide background for other chapters and should be referred to often.

## 9

Profitability Ratios

EXECUTIVE SUMMARY

This chapter discusses two basic types of profitability measures:

- Profitability of investment
- Profitability of sales

The profitability of investment is what we have been referring to as ROI. In this chapter, however, you will see that there are several ways in which this can be calculated:

- Return on total asets (total investment)
- Return on invested capital
- Return on owners' investment

Each of these interpretations provides a different type of information on the profitability of investment. This chapter shows how they are related.

The profitability of sales focuses on specific contributions of purchasing, production, administration, and distribution to overall profitability:

- Gross profit margin
- Operating profit margin
- New profit margin

This chapter shows how to calculate these ratios and what they tell you about effectiveness of cost control at different operating points.

There are two basic types of profitability measures. One type is more general: "How much profit does the company make on each dollar of investment?" The other type simply measures the profitability of sales: "How much profit does the company make on each dollar of sales?" The two measures are related, since both include profits and sales, but there is a significant difference between the two measures in terms of what they tell you.

Profitability of Investment

The first group of ratios focuses on the question: "How well have invested funds been used by the company?"

Return on Assets (ROA)

Profitability of investment is a comprehensive measure of performance, because it considers return on total funds invested. Since total funds invested are equal to total assets held by the company, return on total investment can also be called return on assets (ROA).

The most common form of this ratio is simply net income divided by total investments (or, the same thing, total assets).

$$\text{Return on assets (ROA)} = \frac{\text{Net income}}{\text{Total assets}}$$

$$\text{ROA (19X2)} = \frac{\$90,000}{\$500,000} = .18$$

$$ROA\ (19X1) = \frac{\$87{,}750}{\$452{,}000} = .19$$

Industry norm $= .15$

Evaluation: There has been a slight decrease in performance in 19X2 relative to 19X1. However, the company is still comfortably above the industry norm.

Return on Invested Capital

A problem with the return on assets (ROA) ratio is that it ignores returns to debt investors (that is, the interest payments they receive). The return on invested capital ratio considers not only the net income returns to shareholders but also the interest returns (adjusted for the effect of corporate taxes) on debt.

$$\text{Return on invested capital (RIC)} = \frac{\text{Net income} + \text{interest } (1\text{-}T)}{\text{Interest-bearing debt} + \text{equity}}$$

$$RIC\ (19X2) = \frac{90{,}000 + 20{,}000\ (1\text{-}.5)}{200{,}000 + 175{,}000} = .27$$

$$RIC\ (19X1) = \frac{87{,}750 + 18{,}900\ (1\text{-}.5)}{230{,}000 + 125{,}000} = .27$$

Industry norm $= .23$

Evaluation: Return on total invested capital has not changed. Compared to the industry norm, the company is still significantly higher.

Return on Equity

While the overall effectiveness of management is measured by the return on total assets, other measures of return are also used to focus on particular aspects of return. For example, return on equity (ROE) focuses on the profitability of owners' capital invested, since net income belongs to shareholders.

$$\text{Return on equity} = \frac{\text{Net Income}}{\text{Shareholders equity}}$$

$$ROE\ (19X2) = \frac{9{,}000}{175{,}000} = .51$$

$$\text{ROE (19X1)} = \frac{87,750}{125,000} = .70$$

Industry norm (19X2) = .30

Evaluation: Now a noticeable and important deterioration in profitability is revealed. The profitability of owners' investments (in other words, the return that shareholders earned through the company) has dropped precipitously, although the return is still unusually high. This change will have to be explained. Compared to the industry norm, the company's ROE is still extremely high.

Sales Profitability Ratios

While you should know how much *net income* the company earns on a dollar of sales, this ratio does not tell you everything. For example, what if you want to know how competitive the company's products were? The *gross profit margin* will tell you how much profit the company is making over and above its direct production costs.

Gross Profit Margin

The gross profit margin is calculated by dividing gross profit by the level of sales.

$$\text{Gross Profit Margin} = \frac{\text{Gross Profit}}{\text{Net Sales}}$$

A "high" gross margin indicates that the company's production costs are competitively low or that the company is in a strong enough market position to command higher prices than competitors. A "high" gross margin also indicates that the company can hold its own in a price war or, in the event of an industry recession, how much of a price "buffer" it has relative to competitors.

A "low" gross margin is cause for concern, because it indicates less flexibility in the face of reduced demand or increased competition. Whether you determine that a company's gross margin is "high" or "low," keep in mind that this is only part of the picture. For example, a company might deliberately pursue a low gross margin pricing strategy if it feels that it will significantly increase its market share.

Would you rather have company #1's "high" gross margin and

low sales volume or company #2's "low" gross margin and high sales volume?

	# 1	# 2
Sales	$100	$1,000
Cost of Goods Sold	90	950
Gross Profit	10	50
Gross Margin	10%	5%

Gross Margin Ratios for Tasbem

$$GM \ (19X22) = \frac{\$400,000}{\$1,000,000} = .40$$

$$GM \ (19X1) = \frac{\$386,400}{\$920,000} = .42$$

Industry norm (19X2) = .40

Evaluation: Tasbem's gross margin on sales has decreased by two percentage points between 19X1 and 19X2. Relative to the overall margin of 42 percent in 19X1 this may seem negligible, but it is cause for concern since this will flow all the way through to net profit, where even one percentage point may make an enormous difference. Compared to the industry, Tasbem does not have particularly strong competitive position with respect to pricing.

Operating Profit Margin

This is a ratio of operating profit (earnings before interest and taxes—EBIT) to net sales. Operating profit is derived by deducting operating expenses (such as selling, general, and administrative) from gross profit. The operating margin ignores both interest and taxes. Since interest is affected by the level of debt a company chooses to have (a financial rather than an operating decision) and since a company's taxes are determined by its unique, effective tax status (which may vary widely among companies in the same industry), the operating margin is considered to be a better estimate of the actual sales profitability.

A company with a high operating margin is viewed as stronger and more profitable than one with a low operating margin. Again, however, this opinion must be qualified by a consideration of the volume of activity. A low operating margin on a high volume may be better than a high operating margin on low volume.

$$\text{Operating profit margin} = \frac{\text{Operating profit (EBIT)}}{\text{Net sales}}$$

$$\text{Operating margin (19X2)} = \frac{\$200,000}{\$1,000,000} = .20$$

$$\text{Operating margin (19X1)} = \frac{\$194,400}{\$920,000} = .21$$

$$\text{Industry norm} = .18$$

Evaluation: The reduction of 2 percent in gross profitability (see the gross profit margin) for Tasbem has been cut to only a 1 percent differential in terms of operating profits. In other words, by keeping close control of operating expenses, management has been able to recover some of the ground lost with its weaker gross profit margin.

Compared to the industry norm, Tasbem is still stronger profit-wise. Since Tasbem's gross margin in 19X2 is the same as the industry average, Tasbem's higher operating margin means that its operating expenses are lower than the industry norm.

Profit Margin or Net Profit Margin

This ratio focuses on "the bottom line" and is one of the most popular and heavily emphasized measures of performance. There are, of course, a number of weaknesses in it. I noted earlier that net income is affected by the level of debt a company takes on as well as the unique tax bracket the company may have in a particular year. Furthermore, just as noted with the gross margin and operating margin, profits as a percentage of sales do not provide any information about the volume of activity. A high net profit margin on one unit of sales may be a lot worse than a low net profit margin on thousands of units of sales.

$$\text{Profit margin} = \frac{\text{Net income}}{\text{Sales}}$$

$$\text{Profit margin (19X2)} = \frac{\$90,000}{\$1,000,000} = .09$$

$$\text{Profit margin (19X1)} = \frac{\$87,750}{\$920,000} = .095$$

$$\text{Industry norm (19X2)} = .06$$

Evaluation: The net profitability of sales has been cut by only one-half of a percentage point. Recalling that gross profit margin was down by two percentage points for Tasbem, the recovery of most of this lost ground, resulting in only a .5 percent decrease in profits as a percentage of sales, is gratifying. Still, of course, there is the thought that if its gross margin had been maintained, its net profit margin in 19X2 would actually have been an impressive 11 percent rather than 9 percent! Compared to the industry norm in 19X2, Tasbem is considerably more profitable.

Percentage Analysis

Closely related to the profitability on sales ratios is something called "percentage analysis," also known as "common-size" statements. Instead of focusing only on the various types of profit on the income statement, this method calculates every item on the income statement as a percentage of sales. The usefulness of this type of analysis is that it is easy to compare income statement items from one period to the next and from one company to the next regardless of the actual dollar volumes of sales. If there is a variation in the profitability ratios, the common-size statement will pinpoint the expense categories that most contributed to the variation.

A two-year percentage analysis for the Tasbem Company is presented in Table 9.1.

**Table 9.1. Percentage Analysis for Tasbem Company
for Years Ending 12/31**

		19X2		19X1
Sales		100.0%		100.0%
Cost of goods sold		60.0		58.0
Gross profit		40.0		42.0
Operating expenses:				
Selling	5.0%		5.1%	
Gen'l & admin.	10.0		10.0	
Depreciation	5.0	20.0	5.8	20.9
EBIT		20.0		21.1
Interest		2.0		2.1
Earnings before taxes		18.0		19.0
Taxes (50%)		9.0		9.5
Net income		9.0%		9.5%

Evaluation: In the case of Tasbem, once the percentages are calculated, it is clear that net profit as a percentage of sales has actually dropped, from 9.5 percent to 9.0 percent, even though the dollar amount of profits has increased. The problem appears to be that the cost of goods sold increased from 58 percent to 60 percent of sales (in other words, the gross margin dropped). Management appears to have tried to offset the increased cost of goods sold percentage by increasing output, which decreased operating expenses from 21.1 percent of sales to 20 percent of sales.

## 10

Liquidity Ratios

EXECUTIVE SUMMARY

This chapter explains the role of liquidity in financial management and several ways in which it can be evaluated, including:

- Net working capital
- Current ratio
- Quick ratio

These ratios are only suggestive of the true liquidity position of the company, however, since there are several other potential sources of liquidity available to inside management but not apparent to outsiders, including:

- Credit sources unused but available on short notice
- Liquidation of fixed assets
- Reduction of planned outlays such as capital expenditures

The management of ARC Company (a hypothetical company) was pleased with its performance over recent years:

	19X5	*19X6*	*19X7*	*19X8*	*19X9*	*19YO*
Sales	2,000	4,000	8,000	16,000	32,000	64,000
Net income	200	400	800	1,600	3,200	6,400
Assets	1,000	2,000	4,000	8,000	16,000	32,000

They had been able to double sales and profits each year. Things were looking equally promising for 19Y1, until one day the company ran out of cash. No cash for payrolls; no cash for raw materials; no cash for heat, light, telephone; no cash for the quarterly bank loan payment. No cash, period.

The president called the treasurer. "What the hell happened?"

"No cash," said the treasurer. "Been running out of cash for some time now; late on everything. Suppliers are demanding cash before delivery."

"Then why on God's Green Earth didn't you tell us?" demanded the president.

"Did," said the treasurer. "Often."

"Well, why didn't you get it from the bank?" asked the president.

"Bank won't give us any more," answered the treasurer.

"What do you mean they won't give us any more? Didn't you show them the profits we're generating?"

"I showed them everything. But they said if they put more money into this company, they'll just about own it."

The story about ARC Company is hypothetical, but I am aware of situations in which the "surprises" about cash in this story were just as sudden and just as severe. What I want you to grasp in the ARC Company example is that even profitable companies can run out of cash. This is often a hard thing for financial novices to understand, because intuition tells you that everybody loves a profitable company and that needed expansion funds will always be available if you are profitable enough. But this is erroneous. It is an error of understanding that goes to the heart of this book's mission: The finances of the company do not begin and end with the profit statement. The financing of operations and the assets needed to carry on operations are integral *and usually limited!*

Even profitable companies can't borrow forever. ARC Company

simply ran out of cash because lenders reached their limits, while the company's appetite for cash was voracious. If this appetite cannot be met, operations can come to a grinding halt.

Regardless of how profitable a company ultimately may be, if it cannot raise sufficient cash to meet its obligations (such as the timely payment of debt) and to support operations, the company will be in serious trouble. Operations may have to be cut back or the company may be forced to violate contractual obligations. Thus, the greater its liquidity, the more safety and flexibility a company has. But too much liquidity will result in lower ROI.

Liquidity is measured by a company's cash, marketable securities, and other "near-cash" resources. Near-cash resources include all investments that will be converted into cash within the next twelve months (current assets). Accounts receivable, for example, will be collected; inventory will be sold. As these items get converted into cash, and cash is made available to meet operating requirements, pay maturing debts, make desired investments, exploit unanticipated opportunities, and provide a buffer against operating losses.

In addition to current assets, the company also has available cash resources in the form of unused bank credit, other borrowings that may be available on short notice, and fixed assets that can be sold if necessary. Although these are significant resources for liquidity, they are considered less reliable to external analysts; nor, of course do they show up on the financial statements of the company. For such reasons, measures of liquidity are calculated by outsiders in terms of the current assets possessed by the company as shown on the balance sheet.

Obviously, the balance sheet does not present the true liquidity position of the company, because it is not comprehensive enough and also because the items of immediate interest (current assets and current liabilities) *can change and be changed dramatically on short notice!* Thus, in focusing on balance sheet measures of liquidity, you should interpret the results with caution.

Working Capital or Net Working Capital

One measure of liquidity is net working capital (NWC). This is calculated as total current assets less total current liabilities. It represents the excess of cash resources over requirements anticipated during the next twelve months. Negative net working capital indicates an impending cash shortage.

Net Working Capital = Current Assets-Current Liabilities.

$$\text{NWC (19X2)} = \$250,000 - 125,000 = \$125,000$$
$$\text{NWC (19X1)} = \$202,000 - 100,000 = \$102,000$$

Compared to 19X1, net working capital has improved. This "buffer" has increased from $102,000 to $125,000. But has it increased "enough" relative to the increase in current liabilities? For example, if current liabilities had tripled, would the 25 percent increase in working capital buffer be adequate? The degree of liquidity reflected in the net working capital figure depends a lot on the scale of business. Obviously, net working capital of $125,000 would be dangerously low for a company the size of general Motors. In other words, we have to consider the level of net working capital in relation to the level of current liabilities. This is, in effect, what the *current ratio* does.

Current Ratio

The *current ratio* is a gross measure of liquidity in that it simply compares all liquid assets with all current liabilities. The current ratio is calculated by dividing current assets by current liabilities.

$$\text{Current Ratio} = \frac{\text{Current Assets}}{\text{Current Liabilities}}$$

$$\text{Current Ratio (19X2)} = \frac{250,000}{125,000} = 2.00$$

$$\text{Current Ratio (19X1)} = \frac{202,000}{100,000} = 2.02$$

Industry Norm (19X2) = 2.5

Evaluation: Tasbem's current ratio in 19X2 has not changed noticeably relative to 19X1 but is low compared to the industry norm.

Quick Ratio

An important weakness in the current ratio is the inclusion of inventory as an asset that will be converted to cash within the next twelve months at book value or better. However, if inventory turns out to be unsalable or salable only at a great discount, the measure of liquidity could be misleading. This is especially important since inventories represent a large portion of total current assets.

Inventory investment is subject to greater illiquidity than other current assets. Remember that inventory represents goods not yet sold; accounts receivable, on the other hand, represent legally enforceable claims. Although the full inventory may not be liquidated over the next twelve months, it would be extreme to consider that none of it would be liquidated. In the interest of being conservative, analysts usually calculate the *quick ratio* (also know as the *acid test ratio*) along with the current ratio. The quick ratio is identical to the current ratio with the exception that inventory is omitted from the current assets figure.

$$\text{Quick Ratio} = \frac{\text{Current assets-Inventory}}{\text{Current liabilities}}$$

$$\text{QR (19X2)} = \frac{250{,}000 - 100{,}000}{125{,}000} = 1.20$$

$$\text{QR (19X1)} = \frac{202{,}000 - 80{,}000}{100{,}000} = 1.22$$

Industry norm = 1.50

Evaluation: Tasbem's quick ratio has not changed noticeably in 19X2, but it is still below the industry norm.

11

Financial Structure Ratios

EXECUTIVE SUMMARY

This chapter presents several ratios that shed light on the debt capacity of the company and its level of financial risk. Three ratios are discussed:

- Debt/equity ratio
- Debt/asset ratio
- Interest coverage ratio

A company uses debt in order to reduce the amount of owners' investment required and thus increase the return on owners' investment. This was illustrated in Chapters 8 and 9. The use of debt, however, is a mixed blessing, because it introduces the risk of bankruptcy. Thus, the more debt a company uses, the more financial risk it has.

A company with relatively low levels of debt has flexibility, because it has unused borrowing power that can be tapped, for example, for expansion purposes. A company with relatively high levels of debt has little flexibility, because additional borrowing will be severely limited.

The ratios in this chapter are important to the assessment of the firm's ability to acquire additional funds as well as to the evaluation of the financial strength of the company.

Debt/Equity Ratio

Financial and capital structure ratios are intended to bring out the relative importance of debt financing in the firm and the risks in such financing. Analysts love such ratios.

$$\text{Debt-equity ratio} = \frac{\text{Total liabilities}}{\text{Shareholders' equity}}$$

$$\text{D/E (19X2)} = \frac{325,000}{175,000} = 1.86$$

$$\text{D/E (19X1)} = \frac{327,000}{125,000} = 2.62$$

$$\text{Industry norm} = 1.00$$

Evaluation: Tasbem's proportion of debt financing has dramatically decreased during 19X2. The reduced proportion of debt financing has reduced Tasbem's financial riskiness, and this may be desired by the owners. However, note that Tasbem's debt-to-equity ratio is still considerably higher than the industry norm.

Debt Ratio

Another way of measuring the relative use of debt by a company is to calculate the ratio of total liabilities to total assets. This is known as the company's debt ratio.

$$\text{Total debt ratio} = \frac{\text{Total liabilities}}{\text{Total assets}}$$

$$\text{Debt ratio (19X2)} = \frac{325,000}{500,000} = .65$$

$$\text{Debt ratio (19X1)} = \frac{327,000}{452,000} = .72$$

$$\text{Industry norm} = .50$$

Evaluation: Tasbem's reliance on debt rather than equity financing has dropped substantially in 19X2 relative to 19X1, resulting in much lower financial risk. However, Tasbem's use of debt is still significantly higher than the industry norm.

Coverage Ratios

Coverage ratios focus on the ability of the firm to meet its fixed financial obligations with operating earnings. These debt obligations may be defined as all funds committed to debt interest, debt amortization, lease obligations, and dividend requirements. Often, it is taken to mean simply the coverage of interest payments. These ratios are of particular concern to both the creditors and shareholders.

The *times interest earned ratio* compares the debt interest payments with the operating profits (EBIT) available to meet the interest. It is an attempt to measure how "protected" the interest charge is. This is important, because if the company does not produce enough operating profits to meet the interest payment on debt, the company will be in default on its loan agreement and may be forced to repay the entire borrowing immediately. This ratio is calculated by dividing interest into the operating profits of the company.

$$\text{Times interest earned} = \frac{\text{Operating profits (EBIT)}}{\text{Interest}}$$

$$\text{TIE (19X2)} = \frac{200,000}{20,000} = 10$$

$$\text{TIE (19X1)} = \frac{194,400}{18,900} = 10.3$$

$$\text{Industry norm} = 15.5$$

Evaluation: Despite a large reduction in debt relative to total assets, Tasbem's interest coverage ratio has decreased in 19X2. A coverage ratio of ten times, however, is still quite good. EBIT could drop as much as 90 percent without creating a problem of interest payment. Still, there has been a deterioration in the ratio, and in 19X2 it is significantly lower than the industry norm.

The interest coverge ratio is a very rough estimate of debt service ability for several reasons. For one thing, operating profits are not the same as cash. A company may be very profitable but still may be short of cash. For another thing, debt obligations include repayment of debt principle as well as payment of interest. Failure to come up with enough cash for such other financial requirements will also cause a default and, possibly, an acceleration of the total borrowing. There are more comprehensive coverage ratios which attempt to measure the overall ability to service debt, but they are outside the scope of this book. I will note in passing, however, that any ratios developed will be inferior to detailed projections of cash flows that the company anticipates for purposes of measuring debt capacity.

## 12

Efficiency Ratios

EXECUTIVE SUMMARY

Asset management ratios can provide significant information on the performance of individual managers as well as the company overall. This chapter discusses measures of asset management in three areas:

- Total assets
- Accounts receivable
- Inventory

The efficiency ratios are of prime importance to executive management. The ratios allow top management to analyze performance results and pinpoint the sources of above- or below-expected performance. Such ratios, over time, can alert management to fundamental changes in business activities, such as deterioration in productivity resulting from less efficient equipment. Efficiency ratios can also be used by top management as performance measurement relative to competitors. In this regard, efficiency ratios can also be of great value to investors trying to determine the fundamental soundness of the firm and as a way of anticipating changes in the firm's performance.

Asset Turnover

The asset turnover ratio is a broad measure which reflects the amount of investment needed to support operations. Since such investment must come from the firm's creditors and its owners, this is also an important measure of how productively the invested capital is being used. All else being equal, investors (and top management) would prefer to see high ratios rather than low ones. This ratio must be used with caution, however, since it yields no direct information on profits. A company could generate millions of dollars in sales by simply cutting prices severely, so investors must also be concerned with the profitability of sales when they evaluate a change in asset turnover.

$$\text{Asset turnover} = \frac{\text{Net Sales}}{\text{Total assets}}$$

$$\text{AT (19X2)} = \frac{1{,}000{,}000}{500{,}000} = 2.00$$

$$\text{AT (19X1)} = \frac{920{,}000}{452{,}000} = 2.04$$

$$\text{Industry norm} = 2.50$$

Evaluation: Tasbem's asset turnover has not noticeably changed between 19X1 and 19X2. For both years, however, it has been much less than the industry norm. This is a significant discrepancy and should be further analyzed, since it will have a material impact on ROI. This will become clearer in Chapter 14.

Equity Turnover

Owners are most interested in the "productivity" of their own investment; that is, equity capital to generate a given sales level. Since borrowed money may also be used to generate sales, you must use this ratio with caution because a high ratio may simply reflect an excessive use of borrowed funds.

$$\text{Equity turnover} = \frac{\text{Net sales}}{\text{Shareholders equity}}$$

$$\text{ETO (19X2)} = \frac{1,000,000}{175,000} = 5.71$$

$$\text{ETO (19X1)} = \frac{920,000}{125,000} = 7.36$$

Industry norm = 5.00

Evaluation: The large reduction in equity turnover, from 7.36 times in 19X1 to 5.71 times in 19X2, provides the first strong clue as to why return on shareholders' investment dropped so much even though the profit margin on sales did not. During 19X2, shareholders' investment was not "worked" as intensely as in 19X1. Thus, each dollar of shareholders' investment did not generate as much net income in 19X2 as it did in 19X1. Even so, the turnover rate in 19X2 was higher than that for the industry overall.

Inventory Turnover

This ratio measures the relationship between the investment in inventory and the level or volume of sales. An important question of efficiency in financial management is whether or not the investment in inventory is reflected in increased sales or in an undesirable buildup of slower-moving goods. The most commonly used ratio relates costs of goods sold to the ending inventory.

$$\text{Inventory turnover} = \frac{\text{Cost of goods sold}}{\text{Inventory}}$$

$$\text{ITO (19X2)} = \frac{600,000}{100,000} = 6.0$$

$$\text{ITO (19X1)} = \frac{533,600}{80,000} = 6.67$$

Industry norm (19X2) = 5.0

Note that the numerator is cost of goods sold rather than sales. The reason for using the cost of goods sold figure is that inventories are themselves valued at cost, and it is therefore more appropriate to evaluate the ratio on a cost rather than on a cost plus profit basis. This is known as "true" inventory turnover.

Evaluation: There has been a noticeable slowdown in the turnover of inventory during 19X2. The company is tying up more money in inventory than it did in 19X1. Still, Tasbem's inventory turnover is higher than that for the industry overall.

Average Collection Period

The average collection period provides an estimate of the average age of accounts receivable. It tells us how long, on the average it takes the company to collect its receivables. This is obviously important, since slow-paying customers will increase the level of investment in accounts receivable needed by the firm and thus reduce its overall efficiency of asset use. The average collection period is affected by such factors as the proportion of total sales made on credit and the mix of credit sales. Again, unless there are obvious and important changes in the business, the trend of such estimates is likely to be very informative.

$$\text{Average collection period} = \frac{\text{Accounts receivable}}{\text{Sales per day}}$$

$$\text{Sales per day} = \frac{\text{Sales}}{360}$$

$$\text{ACP (19X2)} = \frac{140,000}{1,000,000/360} = 50.4 \text{ days}$$

$$\text{ACP (19X1)} = \frac{116,000}{920,000/360} = 45.4 \text{ days}$$

$$\text{Industry norm} = 60 \text{ days}$$

Evaluation: Tasbem's average collection period has slowed down, tying up more investment in its credit operations per dollar of sales. However, its average collection period is still better than the industry norm.

## 13

"Market" Value Ratios

EXECUTIVE SUMMARY

This chapter discusses ratios of interest to stockholders, including:

- Earnings per share
- Price/earnings multiple
- Dividend yield
- Dividend payout
- Book value

Several other ratios are often used in financial analysis. Most of them relate to the valuation of the stock. These ratios are of great interest and importance to stockholders.

Earnings Per Share

Although it is dividends rather than earnings that stockholders receive from the company, it is popular to calculate the firm's earnings per share in assessing the value of the stock. This is based on the idea that the fundamental value of a stock lies in the firm's ability to generate earnings from which current and future dividends can be paid. Assume that the company has 100,000 shares outstanding. Earnings per share is calculated simply as:

$$\text{Earnings per share (EPS)} = \frac{\text{Net income}}{\text{Common shares}}$$

$$\text{EPS (19X2)} = \frac{90,000}{100,000} = .90$$

$$\text{EPS (19X1)} = \frac{87,750}{100,000} = .88$$

Evaluation: Earnings for Tasbem have increased slightly despite the decrease in profitability on sales. Yet there has been almost no growth in earnings per share. For a company with high overall profitability (both in 19X1 and in 19X2) we would expect more "performance" in earnings per share. Notice that I have not included an industry comparison. The *level* of EPS for a given company cannot be compared with another company, because EPS can be changed by simply changing the number of shares outstanding. For example, if Tasbem split its stock two for one, there would be 200,000 shares outstanding, each shareholder would have twice as many shares, EPS would "fall" to 45 cents per share, and the price of each share of stock would be half its previous amount. Of course, the company would not be any less valuable simply because it doubled its shares outstanding.

Price/Earnings Multiple

The price/earnings multiple relates the company's current earnings per share to the market value of those earnings. Assume that the company's stock is selling for $10 per share in 19X2 and that it sold for $8 per share at year end 19X1:

$$\text{Price/earnings multiple} = \frac{\text{Market price per share}}{\text{Earnings per share}}$$

$$P/E \ (19X2) = \frac{\$10}{.90} = 11.1 \text{ times}$$

$$P/E \ (19X1) = \frac{\$8}{.88} = 9.1 \text{ times}$$

Industry average = 10.0 times

The P/E multiple is a measure of investor expectation about the prospects of the firm. Relatively *high* P/E multiples indicate investor anticipation of significant growth in earnings of the company or the industry. The industry impact on a company's P/E multiple can be significant. "Good" performers in a bad industry have depressed market values, and vice versa. A relatively *low* multiple suggests less favorable expectations.

Evaluation: The P/E multiple reflects such things as growth in earnings per share. Yet, with almost no growth in earnings, the P/E for Tasbem in 19X2 is much higher than 19X1. The large decrease in return on shareholders' investment (see under "Return on Equity") would normally have a very negative impact on the P/E multiple, but the reverse seems to have occurred.

Tasbem's P/E is higher than the industry average, and this suggests that the company is viewed as a good investment despite its negligible increase in earnings per share.

Dividend Yield

The dividend yield measures the dividend income received by shareholders per dollar of current investment. It is determined by simply dividing the dividend per common share by the current market price per share of the stock. Assume that the company paid a dividend of 40 cents per share in 19X2 and 25 cents per share in 19X1.

$$\text{Dividend yield} = \frac{\text{Dividend per share}}{\text{Market price per share}}$$

$$DY \ (19X2) = \frac{.40}{10} = .04$$

$$DY \ (19X1) = \frac{.25}{8} = .03$$

Industry norm = .04

Evaluation: Tasbem's dividend yield has increased in 19X2 relative to 19X1. Investors like higher dividends, but only if opportunities for profitable reinvestment are limited. Tasbem's new dividend of 40 cents per share is a big increase relative to 19X1. Looking at the industry average, maybe Tasbem has raised its dividend simply to be more in line with the industry average.

Dividend Payout

The level of dividends paid out by a company depends importantly on the level of earnings but also on the availability of profitable investments. Generally speaking, firms that have many profitable opportunities will want to pay out less of their earnings as dividends because they will need the funds for investment. Firms that have fewer profitable investment opportunities and are growing more slowly will need less funds for reinvestment and will therefore pay out more of their profits. The percentage of profits paid out as dividends is called the *payout ratio*.

$$\text{Dividend payout} = \frac{\text{Dividends}}{\text{Net income}}$$

$$\text{PO (19X2)} = \frac{40,000}{90,000} = .44$$

$$\text{PO (19X1)} = \frac{25,000}{87,750} = .28$$

Industry average $= .56$

Evaluation: The dividend payout has increased significantly from 28 percent of earnings to 44 percent of earnings. This means more cash is going out to shareholders. Perhaps Tasbem has more cash than it needs for profitable investments. The stock market has reacted favorably to Tasbem's decision, as its stock price has risen. This explains why the dividend yield on Tasbem's stock has stayed pretty much the same even though dividends per share have increased from 25 cents to 40 cents.

Compared to the industry average, Tasbem is still paying out less of its dividends than the industry overall. The high percentage payout for the industry suggests a mature, low-growth industry.

However, before giving too much weight to the payout ratio let me point out that companies rarely decrease dividends per share, even if profits are down. So a high percentage payout in a given year may simply reflect depressed earnings. The fact that Tasbem's higher payout results from a significant *increase* in dividends rather than a decrease in earnings is more meaningful.

Book Value Per Share

This ratio measures the value of common stock on the assumption that the company is to be liquidated with all the book value on the balance sheet as realizable values. Since investors do not normally buy stock on the assumption that the company is about to be liquidated, the purpose of this calculation is to provide some estimate of the minimum value of the stock. We would normally expect market price per share to be greater than book value per share, but at times stocks may have market prices substantially below their book values per share. Such companies may be said to be "worth more dead than alive." This must be qualified, since it is likely that the common stock market price reflects a more realistic assessment of liquidation value per share. In other words, book values of assets may be overstated relative to realizable sales (liquidation) values.

$$\text{Book value per share} = \frac{\text{Shareholders' equity}}{\text{Common shares outstanding}}$$

$$\text{BV (19X2)} = \frac{175,000}{100,000} = \$1.75$$

$$\text{BV (19X1)} = \frac{125,000}{100,000} = \$1.25$$

Evaluation: Tasbem's book value per share has increased significantly during 19X2. It is interesting to note that its stock price per share is more than five times book value per share. This indicates that investors have a very favorable assessment of the continued profitability of the company.

Summary of Performance

Table 13.1 provides a review of all the applicable ratios for Tasbem as of 19X2 and a brief interpretation of the ratios relative to industry norms as of 19X2.

TABLE 13.1. Summary and Interpretation of Ratios, Tasbem Company, 19X2, Relative to Industry Norm

Ratio	Formula for Calculation	Tasbem (19X2)		Industry Norm	Evaluation
1. PROFITABLITY					
A. *Investment*					
Return on total assets (total investment)	$\dfrac{\text{Net profit after taxes}}{\text{Total assets}}$	$\dfrac{90,000}{1,000,000} =$	.18	.15	Good
Return on invested capital	$\dfrac{\text{Net income} + \text{Interest }(1\text{–}T)}{\text{Interest-bearing debt} + \text{Equity}}$	$\dfrac{90,000 + 10,000}{200,000 + 175,000} =$	.27	.23	Good
Return on owners' investment (equity)	$\dfrac{\text{Income}}{\text{Shareholders' equity}}$	$\dfrac{90,000}{175,000} =$	.51	.30	Very Good
B. *Sales*					
Gross profit margin	$\dfrac{\text{Gross profit}}{\text{Sales}}$	$\dfrac{400,000}{1,000,000} =$	.40	.40	Satisfactory
Operating profit margin	$\dfrac{\text{Operating profit (EBIT)}}{\text{Sales}}$	$\dfrac{200,000}{1,000,000} =$	.20	.18	Good
Net profit margin	$\dfrac{\text{Net income}}{\text{Sales}}$	$\dfrac{90,000}{1,000,000} =$	.09	.06	Very Good
2. LIQUIDITY					
Current Ratio	$\dfrac{\text{Current assets}}{\text{Current liabilities}}$	$\dfrac{250,000}{125,000} =$	2.00	2.50	Weak
Quick Ratio	$\dfrac{\text{Current assets-Inventory}}{\text{Current liabilities}}$	$\dfrac{250,000\text{–}100,000}{125,000} =$	1.20	1.50	Weak

3. FINANCIAL STRUCTURE

Ratio	Formula	Calculation	Result	Benchmark	Assessment
Debt/equity	$\dfrac{\text{Total liabilities}}{\text{Shareholders' equity}}$	$\dfrac{325{,}000}{175{,}000}$	= 1.86	1.00	Weak
Debt/assets	$\dfrac{\text{Total liabilities}}{\text{Total assets}}$	$\dfrac{325{,}000}{500{,}000}$	= .65	.50	Weak
Times interest earned	$\dfrac{\text{EBIT}}{\text{Interest}}$	$\dfrac{200{,}000}{20{,}000}$	= 10.0×	15.5×	Weak

4. ASSET MANAGEMENT

Ratio	Formula	Calculation	Result	Benchmark	Assessment
Total asset turnover	$\dfrac{\text{Sales}}{\text{Total assets}}$	$\dfrac{1{,}000{,}000}{500{,}00}$	= 2.00×	2.50×	Weak
Inventory turnover	$\dfrac{\text{Cost of goods sold}}{\text{Inventory}}$	$\dfrac{600{,}000}{100{,}000}$	= 6.0×	5.0×	Good
Average collection period	$\dfrac{\text{Receivables}}{\text{Sales per day}}$	$\dfrac{140{,}000}{1{,}000{,}000/360}$	= 50.4 days	60.0 days	Good

5. "MARKET" VALUE

Ratio	Formula	Calculation	Result	Benchmark	Assessment
Earnings per share (EPS)	$\dfrac{\text{Net income}}{\text{Common shares}}$	$\dfrac{90{,}000}{100{,}000}$	= .9	not applicable	not applicable
Price/earnings multiple (P/E)	$\dfrac{\text{Market price per share}}{\text{Earnings per share}}$	$\dfrac{\$10}{.9}$	= 11.1	10.0	Good
Dividend yield	$\dfrac{\text{Dividends per share}}{\text{Market price per share}}$	$\dfrac{.40}{\$10}$	= .04	.04	Satisfactory
Dividend payout	$\dfrac{\text{Dividends}}{\text{Net income}}$	$\dfrac{40{,}000}{90{,}000}$	= .44	.56	low
Book value per share	$\dfrac{\text{Shareholders' equity}}{\text{Common shares}}$	$\dfrac{175{,}000}{100{,}000}$	= $1.75	not applicable	not applicable

Qualifications

Now that you have seen how ratios are used, you should be aware of the following qualifications:

 • No matter how sound the techniques may be, if the data analyzed are inaccurate the results are not going to be reliable. The statistical data given in both the balance sheet and the income statement are at best approximations of the real financial operations of a firm.

 • Even large changes in financial variables are meaningless unless the basic reasons for their change can be found. For example, the ratio of net profit to sales may change because of a minor shift in the product mix or changes in the overall economy rather than a change in the competitive position of the firm.

The adjustments of financial statements arising out of these difficulties may be disclosed in the notes to the financial statements, which accompany the regular financial documents. In recent times the greater disclosure of financial and operating information required by the government regulatory agencies, the Securities Exchange Commission and the Federal Trade Commission for example, has helped alleviate the problems mentioned above.

Rarely will all ratios and numerical results yield a consistent pattern for interpretation. As the number of signals and counter-signals increases, the analyst must constantly adjust his evaluation. Analysts must encompass the position, condition, and performance of the firm relative to its objectives and rivals.

Inflation has also had an effect on the interpretation and comparability of ratios.

Inflation and Financial Analysis

Inflation does not have uniform and strictly proportional impacts on a company's financial statements and consequently can bias the results of financial analysis.

To see how inflation affects financial analysis, consider the financial statements in Table 13.2. Assume that these statements precede any inflation.

Impact on Income Statement

Now assume that inflation causes all prices and costs to increase by 10 percent. Sales and operating expenses may increase right away by 10

TABLE 13.2. Financial Statements Before Inflation (in thousands of dollars)

Income Statement

Sales	$1,000
Cost of goods sold (FIFO)	600
Gross profit	400
Operating expenses	60
Depreciation	20
EBIT	320
Interest (@ 10% debt)	20
Earnings before taxes	300
Taxes (50%)	150
Net income	150

Common shares outstanding: 100
Earning per share: $1.50

Balance Sheet

ASSETS		LIABILITIES	
Cash	20	Accounts payable	$300
Accounts receivable	80	Current liabilities	$300
Inventory	600	Long-term debt	200
Current assets	700	Total liabilities	500
Net fixed assets	200	Net worth (shareholders' equity)	400
Total assets	900	Total liabilities & net worth	900

percent each, but cost of goods sold, depreciation, and interest expenses will *not* increase right away since these expenses reflect preinflation conditions (in other words, inventory that was acquired before the rise in inflation; fixed assets acquired before the rise in inflation; and debt that was negotiated before the rise in inflation). In other words, they reflect "historical" rather than current costs of doing business. The income statement will show an increase in net income and earnings per share due to the nonuniform impact of inflation rather than to any fundamental improvement in management performance. (See Table 13.3.)

For example, because of the 10 percent inflation alone, profits have increased by $47, from $150 to $197—an increase of 31 percent!

TABLE 13.3.   Financial Statements After Inflation

Income Statement	
Sales (+ 10%)	$1,100
Cost of goods sold (FIFO—no change)	600
Gross profit	500
Operating expenses (+ 10%)	66
Depreciation (historical—no change)	20
EBIT	414
Interest (historical—no change)	20
Earnings before taxes	394
Taxes (50%)	197
Net Income	$197

\# Common shares outstanding: 100
Earnings per share: $1.92

Note that taxes have also increased by 31 percent from a 10 percent increase in inflation!

Impact on Balance Sheet

Unfortunately, the impact of inflation is not restricted to the income statement. For example, you need 10 percent more cash to handle the same level of operations as before. You also need more investments in accounts receivable (because your prices have increased) and inventory (because the replacement costs are higher). In addition, the cost of replenishing the net fixed assets also has increased. Finally, the interest costs of new debt will now be higher because of inflation.

TABLE 13.4.   Financial Statements After Inflation: Balance Sheet

Assets		*Liabilities and Net Worth*	
Cash (+ 10%)	$22	Accounts payable	$330
Accounts receivable (+ 10%)	88	Current liabilities	330
Inventory (FIFO) (+ 10%)	660	Long-term debt	200
Current assets	770	Total liabilities	530
Net fixed assets	200	Net worth (shareholders' equity)	440
Total assets	970	Total liabilities and shareholders' equity	970

However, because of various lags, the balance sheet will not automatically reflect all of these higher costs of doing business. Cash, accounts receivable, inventory, and accounts payable may show the inflation effects quickly, but the fixed asset and debt accounts will take longer to reflect the impacts of inflation. The short-run impacts are shown in the balance sheet in Table 13.4.

Impact on Ratios

The differential impacts of inflation will bias ratios and may lead to overstating financial performance. This is illustrated in Table 13.5, which shows a number of ratios before and after the impact of inflation.

TABLE 13.5. Effects of Inflation on Selected Ratios

Ratio	Before Inflation	After Inflation
Gross profit margin	40%	45%
Profit margin on sales	15%	18%
Total asset turnover	1.1 times	1.13 times
Return on investment	16.7%	20%
Return on equity	38%	45%
Earnings per share	$1.50	$1.97

## 14

Outline of Performance: Du Pont System

EXECUTIVE SUMMARY

The Du Pont system focuses on the determinants of overall ROI performance. The system is described by means of a chart, which shows that there are two main avenues to ROI improvement: profits per dollar of sales and sales per dollar of investment.

The Du Pont chart used in this book is modified to emphasize particular aspects of profit and investment performance.

The most common form of the Du Pont chart incorporates two potential biases: the amount of debt used and the tax rate applicable.

The ROI calculated in the Du Pont chart measures return on assets (ROA), but it can be easily modified to measure the return on stockholders' investment (ROE) exclusively.

This chapter includes a detailed comparison of performance between two companies.

Figure 14.1 Tasbem ROI Performance, 19X1

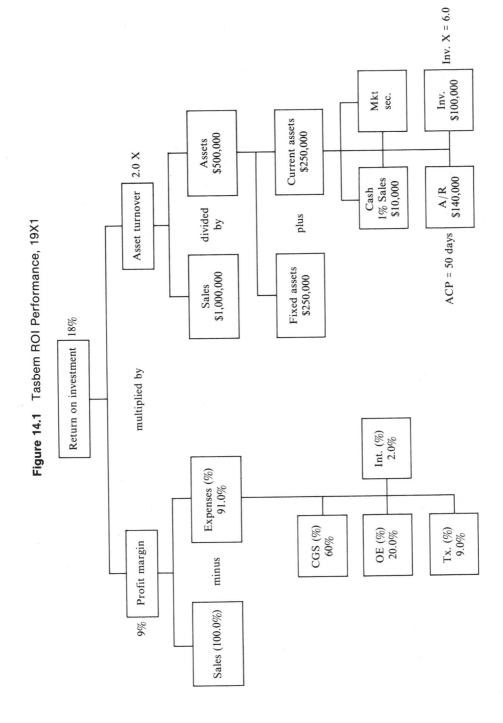

The Du Pont chart (see Figure 14.1) identifies the factors principally responsible for ROI performance. It also allows a ready comparison of these factors among companies, for the same company over time, or for a company against established targets. The example below uses a modified form of the Du Pont chart to analyze data developed for Tasbem.

The chart resembles a pyramid. The top of the pyramid represents ROI. The farther down the pyramid, the more specific the contributing areas to performance become.

The chart illustrates what I have been stressing: overall ROI is mutually determined by profitability on sales (profit margin) and the rate of investment (asset) turnover. Tasbem's ROI of 18 percent represents a profit margin of 9 percent and an investment turnover rate of 2 times. In other words, if investment turnover had been 3.0 times, ROI would have been 27 percent instead of 18 percent. If the sales margin had been 10 percent, ROI would have been 20 percent.

$$ROI = PM \times ATO$$
$$18\% = 9\% \times 2.0$$

The profit margin and turnover rates, of course, are the results of numerous other variables. For example, the profit margin is affected by the relationships of all expenses to sales; the investment turnover rate is affected by the individual turnover rates of all the investment components. Therefore, the profit margin and turnover figures should be further broken down among the rest of the components.

The profit margin results can be taken directly from the percentage analysis statement shown in Table 9.1. Total investment turnover can be broken down into the turnover of working capital investments and fixed asset investments. Working capital investments include all the current asset items: accounts receivable and inventory levels as well as cash.

How to "Read" the Du Pont Chart

The ROI of 18 percent resulted from a profit margin of 9 percent and a turnover of investment of 2 times. The profit margin of 9 percent resulted from cost of goods sold of 60 percent, operating expenses of

20 percent, interest expenses of 2 percent, and tax expense of 9 percent of sales.

The turnover of investment of 2.0 times represented a turnover of fixed assets of 4 times and a turnover of current assets of 4 times. The current asset turnover resulted from an average collection period of fifty days, which resulted in accounts receivable of $140,000. Inventory turnover was 6 times (based on cost of goods sold) and contributed $100,000 to total assets.

How to "Interpret" the Du Pont Chart

Interpretations are not possible without standards of comparison, like those suggested for ratio analysis. Let's interpret Tasbem's performance from two perspectives: a "what if" perspective to show how the changes in individual variables affect ROI, and a comparison between Tasbem and Rival (its major competitor).

"What If" Analysis

In order to develop more of a familiarity with the ROI model, examine what impact on ROI will follow from specific improvements in profitability and efficiency. For example, if cost of goods sold had been two percentage points lower (i.e., 58 percent instead of 60 percent), the pretax profit margin would have been 2 percent higher and (after the IRS would have taken its share), net income would have been 1 percent higher (i.e., 10 percent of sales instead of 9 percent of sales). With Tasbem's turnover of 2 times, ROI would have been 20 percent instead of 18 percent. By similar reasoning, a decrease in operating expenses of 1 percent would have increased the profit margin by 0.5 percent (to 9.5 percent), and overall ROI would have been 19 percent.

Impact of a Decrease in Average Collection Period

A reduction in assets, for the same sales volume, will decrease the investment tied up and, therefore, raise ROI. A decrease in the average collection period has the effect of reducing accounts receivable investment. This will increase asset turnover and ROI.

If Tasbem's average collection period drops from 50.4 days of sales to 30 days of sales, accounts receivable will be:

$$A/R = \text{Avg. collection period} \times \text{Sales per day}$$
$$= 30 \times \frac{\$1,000,000}{360}$$
$$= \$83,333$$

instead of $140,000, or a decrease of $56,667 in required investment. Total assets will be $56,667 lower, or, $443,333, which on a sales volume of $1,000,000 would represent a turnover of 2.26 times instead of the 2.0 actually achieved. ROI would therefore have been 20.3 percent instead of 18 percent—purely as a result of lower accounts receivable investment, a shortened collection period.

Impact of an Increase in Inventory Turnover

Similarly, lower inventory levels increase inventory turnover, which results in higher total asset turnover.

If inventory turnover had been 10 times instead of 6 times, inventory investment would have been $60,000 instead of $100,000 (or, $40,000 lower). Total assets would have been $40,000 lower, or, $460,000. This would have increased investment turnover to 2.17, and ROI would have increased to 19.6 percent instead of 18 percent.

Impact of Combined Decreases in
Accounts Receivable and Inventory

If both accounts receivable and inventory investment can be reduced, the impact on ROI is, of course, larger.

If accounts receivable had been kept to 30 days and inventory had been kept to a turnover of 10 times, total assets would have been $96,667 lower (i.e. $56,667 + $40,000) or, $403,333. Total turnover would have been 2.5 times, producing an ROI of 22.3 percent instead of the 18 percent actually realized!

Comparison with Rival

On the basis of overall ROI (see Figure 14.2), Tasbem and Rival appear to have done equally well. But have they performed equally well in all areas? A comparison based on the Du Pont system reveals that the two companies performed differently in profitability and in the efficiency of asset use.

Rival's profit performance of 12 percent was much better than Tasbem's 9 percent. But Rival's asset turnover of 1.5 was much lower than Tasbem's. To better understand these differences in performance, we need to look farther down the pyramid. There are important differences along both the profitability and the turnover branches.

Cost of Goods Sold

Rival had much cheaper costs of production per dollar of sales as indicated by its cost of goods sold of 56 percent of sales as against 58 percent for Tasbem. Reasons for this are not obvious but this is clearly an area for further probing.

	Cost of Goods Sold
Tasbem	58%
Rival	56%

Operating Expenses

In this area too, Rival has outperformed Tasbem noticeably. We should keep in mind that operating expenses contain some semivariable and fixed cost components. Thus, Rival's much greater volume of sales may be yielding some ''economies of scale'' by decreasing operating expenses per dollar of sales.

	Operating Expenses
Tasbem	20.9%
Rival	18.0%

Interest Expense

There is no significant difference in this cost item as a percentage of sales.

Figure 14.2 Tasbem (19X1) vs. Rival (19X1)

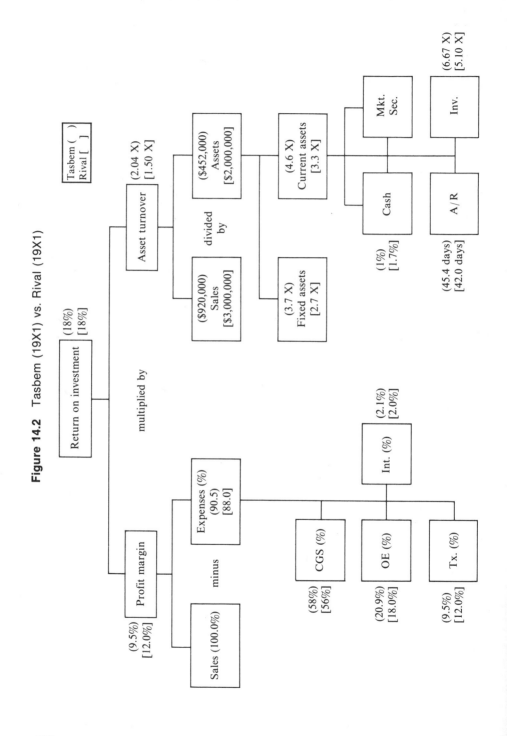

Pretax Profits

We have more narrowly focused the performance differential, almost 3 percentage points of Rival's lower costs is due to efficiencies in operating expenses and 2 percentage points arise from lower costs of production per dollar of sales.

Taxes

Greater profits lead to greater taxes as a percentage of sales, and this is true for Rival. Half of its pretax improvement is paid to the IRS, resulting in more taxes per dollar of sales for Rival than for Tasbem.

	Taxes
Tasbem	9.5%
Rival	12.0%

Asset Use

What RIVAL gained in profitability as a percentage of sales, it appears to have lost with a much slower asset turnover, suggesting lower productivity of investment per dollar of sales generated.

	Total Asset Turnover
Tasbem	2.04 ×
Rival	1.50 ×

Rival's asset turnover was lower, but was this because of less effective use of fixed investment, of current investment, or both? To understand this better, we need to look at the turnover rates separately.

Fixed Asset Turnover

Rival's fixed asset turnover was only 2.7 times, compared to 3.7 times for Tasbem, and this has hurt Rival's overall ROI. But has it explained the entire difference in asset efficiency?

	Fixed Asset Turnover
Tasbem	3.7 ×
Rival	2.7 ×

Notice that if Rival had also experienced a fixed asset turnover of 3.7 times, its $3,000,000 in total sales would have required only $811,000 in fixed assets instead of the $1,000,000 actually committed.

Current Asset Turnover

Rival's turnover of current assets is also weaker than Tasbem's. Rival's current asset turnover is 3.3 times, compared with 4.6 times for Tasbem.

	Current Asset Turnover
Tasbem	4.6 ×
Rival	3.3 ×

If Rival's use of working capital (current assets) had been as productive as Tasbem's, only $652,000 in current assets would have been required, rather than the $900,000 actually used.

Beyond these observations, we can also note in the comparison that Rival had almost twice as much tied up in cash and marketable securities (1.7 percent of sales) as Tasbem (1 percent of sales), and a turnover of inventory of only 5.1 times compared with 6.7 times for Tasbem. However, Rival did show slightly better credit experience with an average collection period of only 42 days compared with 45.4 days for Tasbem.

Overall Evaluation of Asset Use

Overall, Rival has almost $500,000 more in assets than necessary if it had the same efficiency as Tasbem. However, before concluding that Rival's management has been inferior in the use of assets, we have to reconcile the poorer asset performance with the much better operating performance. For example, what if Rival's greater fixed asset investment reflects purchase of more efficient equipment, thereby reducing cost of goods sold? I will stress this in more detail in following chapters, but the point is worth emphasizing here also. By increasing capital investment a company may be able to widen its gross profit margin. However, even though this may lead to greater profits, greater investment is also involved—thus ROI may actually decrease! Again, for such reasons the overall ROI estimate, combining both asset efficiency and operating performance, is a better measure of overall management effectiveness.

Two Important Biases in the ROI Chart

The popular form of the Du Pont method, which I have just illustrated, is vulnerable to two important biases. One of these arises when we compare companies with different levels of debt in the capital structure. The company with the higher debt use will show greater interest expense and thus a lower profit margin on sales and a lower ROI.

Assume that company 1 has no debt and company 2 is almost completely debt-financed. In all other respects, companies 1 and 2 have exactly the same sales, profits, and assets. The relevant data are summarized below.

	1	*2*
Sales	$1,000,000	$1,000,000
CGS	600,000	600,000
Gross profit	400,000	400,000
Oper. expenses	200,000	200,000
EBIT	200,000	200,000
Interest	0	40,000
EBT	200,000	160,000
Taxes	100,000	80,000
Net income	100,000	80,000
Assets	500,000	500,000
Debt	0	400,000
Shareholders' equity	500,000	100,000
Profit margin	10%	8%
Asset turnover	2	2
ROI	20%	16%

According to the Du Pont method, company 1 has done better than company 2. Yet the only difference between the two is that company 2 used a lot of debt while 1 used no debt. Was company 2 foolish to incur debt? No. Company 2 deliberately undertook debt financing to reduce the required investment by shareholders. In other words, company 2 is more concerned with increasing the returns to the owners. We will soon see how to adjust for this and the following weakness.

Different Tax Rates

A company in a higher tax bracket will lose a bigger share of pretax profits to the IRS than a company in a lower tax bracket. Because of these tax bracket differentials a company might seem less profitable simply because it is in a higher tax bracket. When evaluating a company's performance, the potential distortion of differential tax brackets should be recognized.

For example, assume that company 2 had losses in previous years which, in the current year, resulted in a zero tax liability. Its taxes would have been 0 instead of 80, and its profit margin would have been 16 percent instead of 8 percent of sales. With its turnover of 2.0, company 2's ROI would have been 32 percent, compared to company 1's 20 percent. An impressive performance for a company that had previously been unprofitable.

Correcting for the Biases

The simplest way to correct the Du Pont approach for the biases that arise from differentials in taxes and debt usage is to calculate the ROI on the basis of operating income, EBIT rather than after taxes as a percentage of sales.

	1	*2*
Sales	$1,000,000	$1,000,000
EBIT	200,000	200,000
Oper. Profit Margin	20%	20%
Assets	500,000	500,000
Turnover	2.0	2.0
ROI (EBIT)	40%	40%

We now have a more valid picture of operating performance, unbiased by differentials in debt usage or tax rates, and, as we already knew, there was no basic difference between the two companies.

Performance from the Shareholders' View

Companies undertake debt financing to reduce the level of share-holders' investment required and therefore to increase the profitability of shareholders' investment.

In previous examples, company 2 had less profits than company 1 but also a lot less owner's investment required. Therefore, the return on owner's investment was magnified in company 2.

	1	*2*
Net income	$100,000	$80,000
Shareholders' equity	500,000	100,000
ROE	20%	80%

In the context of my Du Pont chart we would guess that the turn-over of equity investment was much higher for company 2.

	1	*2*
Sales	$1,000,000	$1,000,000
Shareholders' equity	500,000	100,000
Equity turnover	2.0	10.0

And ROE is equal to the profit margin on sales times the equity turn-over.

	1	*2*
PM	10%	8%
Equity turnover	2.0	10.0
ROE	20%	80%

Reporting to a Higher Authority: Return on Equity

Return on shareholders' investment is related to the return on invest-ment as calculated in the simplified Du Pont chart in the following way:

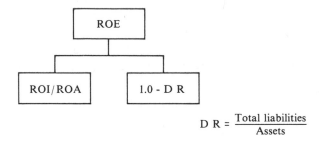

$$D R = \frac{\text{Total liabilities}}{\text{Assets}}$$

In other words, return on equity is equal to return on investment (i.e. ROE = ROI) only when all investment is financed with shareholders' equity (i.e., there is no debt). As a company increases its use of debt relative to equity, the debt/asset ratio will rise, and this will increase return on equity. However, there is an additional effect of debt that must be recognized. As debt use increases, interest expense increases, which will reduce the firm's profit margin. The final effect of debt use on the return on equity, therefore, depends on the relationship between the interest rate on debt and the profitability of sales.

Profit Management

This part contains the following chapters:

There are only two types of actions that management can take to increase ROI:

- Increase profits per dollar of sales
- Decrease investment per dollar of sales

This part focuses on techniques for estimating profits, developing profit objectives, and ensuring success of the profit plan.

In order to estimate and develop profit objectives, an understanding of the cost-volume-profit relationships in the company is necessary. This is taken up in Chapter 15, which deals with break-even analysis, and Chapter 16, which deals with leverage analysis.

The development of financial plans is discussed in Chapter 17, which deals with pro forma statements. Chapter 18, which addresses the financial limits to growth, provides an insight into the feasibility of profit objectives. Chapter 19 describes the role of the cash budget as an effective technique for managing the profit plan.

15

Break-Even Analysis

EXECUTIVE SUMMARY

Whenever a company has fixed costs to cover, break-even analysis is appropriate. Break-even analysis ties together the price-cost characteristics of the company to determine the minimum volume of sales needed to avoid losses. In this sense, it is a form of "worst case" analysis.

Break-even analysis is also used for sensitivity analysis of different price-cost-sales assumptions. For example, it can be used to examine alternative pricing decisions and share-of-market assumptions.

Since break-even analysis identifies the minimum output level needed to avoid losses, it is sometimes used as an input to investment decisions. For example, the analysis of proposed new products will include estimates of break-even sales and market share. Break-even analysis is also used in deciding whether to

113

change the type of production costs. For example, it is used to examine the effect of replacing manual labor with machines.

The principle strengths of break-even analysis are:

- Little information required
- Easy to calculate
- Useful approximation over short run
- Easily understood
- Easy to revise

The principle limitations of break-even analysis are:

- Prices and costs not stable
- Not useful for long run
- Unreliable for multiproduct analysis
- Unreliable for large variation in output
- Assumes sales equals production
- Hard to classify costs as either variable or fixed
- Ignores ROI

Break-even analysis focuses on the price-cost-sales characteristics of individual products and lines of business. Break-even analysis is applied in three main areas:

- Risk analysis
- Pricing decisions
- Production decisions

Risk Analysis

Break-even analysis is used to determine the minimum sales level needed to avoid losses. When the break-even sales volume is compared to the actual or expected sales volume, you can get some idea of the loss potential.

Let's say that you are considering a new product, product # 5. You have decided that a price of $4.50 per unit will be competitive. Variable costs of production are expected to be $2.50 per unit, and fixed costs will be $60,000 per year.

With the estimated price-cost relationships, a minimum of 30,000 units will have to be sold per year to avoid losses. Since the minimum required sales level is about half the projected sales volume in the first year, the risk level is considered to be tolerable.

Pricing Decisions

The price set for a product determines not only the quantity that can be sold but also the break-even point.

Let's say that at a price of $3.00 per unit sales of product # 5 can be increased dramatically. With the same cost relationships, however, the break-even volume will rise to 120,000 units per year, or about double the sales volume anticipated at a price of $4.50 per unit.

Alternatively, if you set a price of $6.00 per unit, with the same cost relationships, the break-even sales volume will be only slightly over 17,000 units. Of course, the higher sales price will mean a less competitive product.

Production Decisions

Break-even analysis is sometimes used in selecting among production methods involving different combinations of variable and fixed costs. The "make-or-buy" decision is an important version of such a decision.

Let's say you are considering whether to buy finished frisbees for resale or whether to manufacture them yourself.

If you buy finished frisbees, your break-even sales level will be 20,000 units per year. If you make them youself, your break-even sales level will be 30,000 units per year. Relative to expected sales of 40,000 per year, it will be much safer to purchase finished frisbees.

However, from what you have learned so far, you should recognize the fact that break-even analysis is not a reliable guide to investment decisions, because it completely ignores ROI. Break-even analysis is helpful in making investment decisions insofar as it provides information about risk—but that's about it!

The Break-Even Chart

Figure 15.1 shows a typical break-even chart for the Life Co. The break-even point (B/E) represents the level of sales at which total

Figure 15.1   Life Company Break-Even Chart

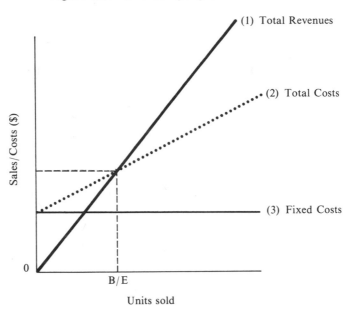

revenues just equal total costs. On the chart, the break-even point is determined by the intersection of the total revenue and total cost lines.

The *total revenue* line is simply price times the number of units sold: no sale, no revenues. Higher prices yield more total revenues for each level of sales. The total revenue line becomes steeper, producing a lower break-even point.

The *total cost* line is made up of *fixed costs* and *variable costs*. At a sales level of zero units, variable costs are zero so total costs are equal to fixed costs. *Total variable costs* are equal to variable costs per unit times the number of units sold. The variable cost portion of total costs is equal to the difference between total costs and fixed costs.

How to Calculate the Break-Even Point

The first thing you have to do is analyze the costs associated with the product you are considering. The costs have to be classified into one of two categories:

- Variable costs
- Fixed costs

Figure 15.2 Variable Costs

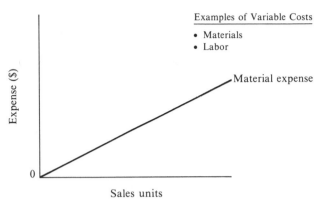

Variable Costs

Variable costs vary in proportion to changes in sales. When sales are zero, variable costs are zero. Figure 15.2 shows what a variable cost looks like.

Fixed Costs

Fixed costs do not vary in any systematic way with changes in sales. Actually, fixed costs can and will change from time to time, but not as a direct result of changes in sales. In other words, fixed costs are insensitive to fluctuations in sales. Figure 15.3, shows what a fixed cost looks like.

Figure 15.3 Fixed Costs

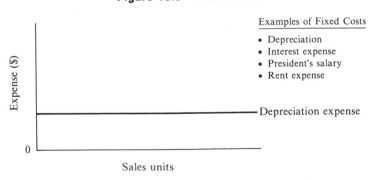

Figure 15.4   Semivariable Cost—General and Administrative Expense

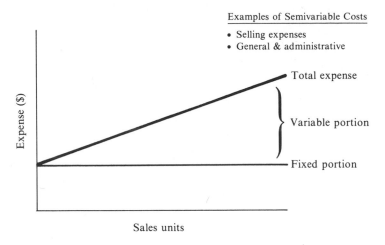

Semivariable Costs

Semivariable costs contain elements of variable and fixed costs. In other words, some part of semivariable costs fluctuates with variation in sales, and some part is insensitive to fluctuations in sales. The components of semivariable costs can usually be estimated by looking at

Table 15.1.   Income Statement for the Year Ending December 31, 19X2

			Variable	*Fixed*
Sales (100,000 units @ $10/unit)		$1,000,000		
Cost of goods sold		600,000	$600,000	
Gross profit		400,000		
Operating expenses:				
Selling	50,000		30,000	$20,000
Gen'l & admin.	100,000		20,000	80,000
Depreciation	50,000	200,000		50,000
Operating profit (EBIT)		200,000		
Nonoperating expenses: Interest		20,000		20,000
Earnings before taxes		180,000		
Taxes (50%)		90,000		
Net income		90,000		
Total			$650,000	$170,000

the total cost (for example, selling) over time and seeing how it has changed with different sales volumes. The level of semivariable cost associated with zero sales volume is considered to be the fixed part; increases over this fixed part are variable. The components of semivariable costs are illustrated in Figure 15.4.

Assume you have decided that the expense breakdown shown in Table 15.1 is reasonable. Note that since you are concerned with break-even, you are not concerned with items below the "Earnings before taxes" line. Obviously, at the break-even level earnings before taxes will be zero. In the example, total variable costs are $650,000 on a volume of 100,000 units, or $6.50 per unit. Total fixed costs are $170,000.

Notice that at a price of $10 per unit, $6.50 is automatically absorbed as variable costs, regardless of the level of sales. Thus, on every unit sold, there is a net of $3.50 available to meet fixed costs and profits, if any. The $3.50 is the available *contribution per unit*. In order to determine the break-even level of sales, you simply divide total fixed costs by the contribution per unit of output:

$$\text{Break-even units} = \frac{\text{Fixed costs}}{\text{Contribution per unit}}$$
$$= \frac{\$170,000}{\$3.50} = 48,571 \text{ units}$$

Checking the Break-Even Point

Sales of 48,571 units at $10 per unit will produce total revenues of $485,710. Cost of goods sold are 60 percent of sales, so they will be $291,426.

$$\text{Cost of goods sold} = .60 \times \$485,710 = \$291,426$$

Gross profit will be equal to total sales less cost of goods sold, or $194,284.

Selling expenses are partly variable and partly fixed. These are made up of $20,000 in fixed expenses and a variable portion which is 3 percent of total sales. Thus, selling expenses at the break-even volume will be:

$$\text{Selling espenses} = \$20,000 + (.03 \times \$485,710)$$
$$= \$34,571$$

General and administrative expense is also semivariable. There is a fixed expense of $80,000 plus a variable portion equal to 2 percent of total sales. At the break-even, then, total general and administrative expense will be:

General & administrative expenses = $80,000 + (.02 × $485,710)
= $89,714

Depreciation expense is completely fixed, so it will stay at $50,000 even at the break-even level of sales.

Interest Expense

I am treating interest expense as completely fixed for this analysis. Therefore, it will remain at $20,000 even at the break-even level of sales.

Combining the Break-Even Estimates

You now have all the information needed for developing a hypothetical income statement at the break-even level of sales:

Sales (48,571 units @ $10)	$485,710
Cost of goods sold (60% of sales)	291,426
Gross profit	194,284
Operating expenses:	
Selling ($20,000 + 3% of sales)	34,570
Gen'l & Admin ($80,000 + 2% of sales)	89,714
Depreciation	50,000
	174,284
Operating profit	20,000
Interest expense	20,000
Earnings before taxes	0

Advantage of Fixed Costs

Since fixed costs usually raise the break-even sales level—and thus the risks associated with particular products—you might wonder why companies don't try to avoid them. The reason fixed costs are attractive is that beyond the break-even sales level, the fixed costs result in greater profits per dollar of sales and therefore higher profit margins and higher ROI!

The impact of fixed costs on the sales profit margin is revealed in leverage analysis, which is taken up in the next chapter.

## 16

Leverage Analysis

EXECUTIVE SUMMARY

Leverage has the effect of magnifying a percentage change in sales into a larger percentage change in profits and earnings per share. If the change in sales is positive, leverage is beneficial. If sales decrease, leverage will hurt.

Leverage exists whenever a company has fixed costs. There are two basic types of fixed costs: operating and financial. Operating leverage magnifies a percentage change in sales into a larger percentage change in operating profits. Financial leverage takes up where operating leverage leaves off: It magnifies a percentage change in operating profits into a larger percentage change in profits and earnings per share.

The total or combined leverage for a company is equal to the product of operating and financial leverages.

The *degree* of leverage is a relative measure of the leverage a company has. The degree of operating leverage tells you how large a change in operating profit will result from a given percentage change in sales. The degree of financial leverage tells you how large the change in earnings per share will result from a given percentage change in EBIT. The degree of combined leverage incorporates both operating and financial leverage effects. It tells you how large the change in earnings per share will result from a given percentage change in sales.

Leverage analysis is of obvious help in profit planning and is also used in budgeting, risk analysis, pricing, production decisions, and financing decisions. Leverage analysis is really just an extension of break-even analysis and employs the same basic information as break-even analysis: price, quantity, variable cost, fixed cost.

Uses:

- Aid in selecting among production methods
- Pricing decisions
- Output decisions
- Risk analysis
- Profit planning
- Budget preparation/cost control
- Financing decisions

Strengths:

- Little information needed
- Easy to calculate
- Easily understood
- Easy to revise
- Estimate effects of decisions before they are made

Limitations:

- Prices and costs not stable
- Not useful for long run
- Unreliable for multiproduct analysis
- Unreliable for large variation in output
- Assumes sales equal production

- Hard to classify costs as either variable or fixed
- Ignores ROI

Leverage analysis focuses on the profit impact of fixed costs. There are two types of fixed costs (operating and financial), and each has a distinct leverage effect. Operating leverage magnifies the impact of a change in sales on operating profits (EBIT). Financial leverage magnifies the impact of a change in operating profits on net income and earnings per share (EPS). Total leverage for a company magnifies the impact of a change in sales on net income and EPS.

Leverage Relationships on Income Statement

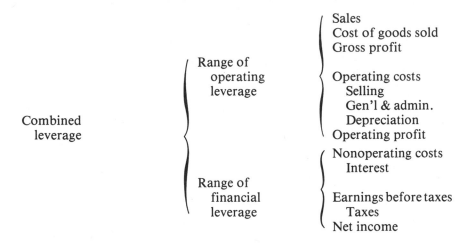

Degree of Operating Leverage

The degree of operating leverage (DOL) tells you how much of an impact of EBIT will result from a percentage change in sales. A firm with *no* operating leverage has a DOL equal to 1.00: In other words, without leverage there is *no* magnification on EBIT from a change in sales. Operating income changes by the same percentage as sales.

Let's say a company has no operating leverage, so its DOL is 1.00. This means that a 10 percent increase in sales will produce a 10 percent increase in EBIT. A 15 percent decrease in sales will produce a 15 percent decrease in EBIT.

Let's now say DOL is 2.0. This means that the change in EBIT will be twice as large as the change in sales. If sales increase 10 percent, operating profit will increase 20 percent. If sales decrease 15 percent, EBIT will decrease 30 percent.

Degree of Financial Leverage

The degree of financial leverage (DFL) tells you how sensitive net income and EPS are to changes in operating income (EBIT). A firm with *no* financial leverage will have a DFL equal to 1.00.

A company has DFL of 3.00. If EBIT increases by 20 percent, net income and EPS will increase by 60 percent. If EBIT decreases by 30 percent, net income and EPS will decrease by 90 percent.

Degree of Combined Leverage

The degree of combined leverage (DCL) combines the impacts of DOL and DFL. It tells you how sensitive net income and EPS are to changes in sales. DCL is equal to DOL *times* DFL for reasons which will become clearer below. A DCL equal to 1.00 means that the company has no leverage (no fixed costs) at all.

If DOL is 2.00 and DFL is 3.00, DCL is 6.00. If sales increase 10 percent, net income and EPS will increase 60 percent. If sales decrease 15 percent, net income and EPS will decrease 90 percent. (These numbers coincide with those above.)

In other words, notice that if DOL is 2.00, DFL is 3.00, and sales increase 10 percent, EBIT will increase by 20 percent. If EBIT increases by 20 percent, given a DFL of 3.00, net income will increase by 60 percent. If sales decrease by 15 percent, EBIT will decrease by 30 percent. If EBIT decreases by 30 percent, net income will decrease by 90 percent.

The degree of leverage is not constant for a company. It depends on, among other things, the level at which the firm is operating. For a given level of fixed costs, variable costs per unit, and selling price per unit, the degree of leverage is always greatest when the company is at its break-even level of operation. As the company's sales volume increases above its break-even point, the degree of leverage diminishes.

Like break-even analysis, leverage analysis is fundamentally a short-run perspective and assumes that estimated relationships (prices per unit, variable cost per unit, and fixed costs) will be stable.

Leverage analysis is of obvious help in profit planning and is also used in budgeting, risk analysis, pricing decisions, production decisions, and financing decisions. Leverage analysis is really just an extension of break-even analysis and employs the same basic information as break-even analysis: price, quantity, variable cost, fixed costs.

Profit Planning

Leverage analysis can be very helpful in profit planning. For example, you may be committed to a certain minimum increase in net income and earnings per share. Leverage analysis will tell you what increase in sales volume will be necessary to meet the profit objective.

If your calculated overall leverage is 2.0 and you are committed to an increase of 20 percent in profits and earnings per share during the coming year, you will need to increase sales volume by about 10 percent.

Risk Analysis

Leverage analysis permits an estimate of the downside risk resulting from a decrease in sales volume. Assume that your overall (DCL) leverage rate is 3.0. A decrease in sales volume of 10 percent will produce a 30 percent reduction in net profits and earnings per share.

Production Decisions

In selecting among production methods with different combinations of variable cost and fixed costs, leverage analysis provides important information about the volatility of profits. However, it is important to recognize that leverage analysis focuses on *profits* rather than ROI. Therefore, it is *not* a proper or reliable guide to investment decisions. A classic example of this type of choice is the decision whether to automate a manual production process.

Process #1 is all hand-assembled. Process #2 is all machine-assembled. Parts to be assembled (variable costs) are the same in both processes and cost $2 per unit. Labor for process #1 is $5 per unit. Depreciation on the machine used for process #2 is $500,000 per year. Price of the output is $10 per unit. At a sales level of 100,000 units, both processes produce the same profit. But, to emphasize, process #2 will require much more investment. Therefore ROI for process # 2 is much lower at the $1,000,000 sales level.

	# 1	# 2
Sales @ $10	$1,000,000	$1,000,000
Material and factory overhead expense @ $2	200,000	200,000
Labor expense @ $5	500,000	0
Depreciation	0	500,000
EBIT	300,000	300,000
DOL =	1.0	2.67

Process # 1 has no fixed costs, hence no leverage. DOL is equal to 1.00. Process # 2 has a DOL of 2.67, a high degree of leverage.

If sales increase by 10 percent, EBIT for process # 1 will increase by 10 percent. But EBIT for process # 2 will increase by 26.7 percent.

	# 1	# 2
Sales (110,000 units @ $10)	$1,100,000	$1,100,000
Material and factory overhead expense @ $2	220,000	220,000
Labor expense @ $5	550,000	0
Depreciation	0	500,000
EBIT	330,000	380,000
% change in sales	+ 10%	+ 10%
% change in EBIT	+ 10%	+ 26.7%

Financing Decisions

In contrast to DOL, a company has much more discretion over its DFL. Fixed financial expenses arise from the use of debt. A firm with no debt will have no financial leverage. The DFL is thus an indication of financial risk in a company. There are limits to the amount of debt a company can carry or, for that matter, secure, but there is still considerable management discretion over this type of risk. The level of financial risk assumed is necessarily influenced by the level of operating risk in the company and by its DOL.

Assume that if process # 1 is used a lot of debt financing is available but if process # 2 is used, no debt financing is available. Process # 1 will require a lot less investment by owners than will process # 2.

For clarity, assume that interest on the debt financing is $188,000.

	# 1	# 2
EBIT	$300,000	$300,000
Interest	188,000	0
EBT	112,000	300,000
Taxes (50%)	56,000	150,000
Net income	56,000	150,000
DFL =	2.67	1.00

Ignore the fact that profits for # 1 are a lot lower than for # 2. (Remember that # 1 has a much lower investment required from owners). The important thing to note is that DFL for process # 1 is 2.67 and the DFL for # 2 is 1.00, just the reverse of the DOL relationship. It's clear that the DCL for both processes will be the same.

	# 1	# 2
DOL =	1.00	2.67
DFL =	2.67	1.00
DCL =	(1.00) × (2.67)	(2.67) × (1.00)
	= 2.67	2.67

In other words, a change in sales will have the same impact on net income for both processes. To see this, let's complete the income statement used earlier, assuming a 10 percent increase in sales volume.

	# 1	# 2
Sales (110,000 units @ $10)	$1,100,000	$1,100,000
Materials factory overhead @ $2	220,000	220,000
Labor @ $5	550,000	0
Depreciation	0	500,000
EBIT	330,000	380,000
Interest	188,000	0
EBT	142,000	380,000
Taxes (50%)	71,000	190,000
Net income	71,000	190,000
% change in sales	+ 10%	+ 10%
% change in net income =	$71,000 − 56,000 / 56,000	$190,000 − 150,000 / 150,000
=	26.7%	26.7%

How to Calculate Degree of Operating Leverage

Let's break up the income statement on page 118 into fixed and variable costs, just as we did with break-even analysis. Remember the uncertainty about the components of semivariable expenses. Since the degree of leverage is sensitive to the level of sales, we also need to know how many units of sales we are talking about. DOL is a simple ratio. The numerator has the contribution per unit (i.e., price minus variable cost) times the number of units projected. This is the same thing as total dollar contribution. The denominator is simply EBIT.

$$\text{DOL} = \frac{(\text{Quantity}) \times (\text{Price minus variable cost per unit})}{\text{EBIT}}$$

$$= \frac{(100,000) \times (\$10. - \$6.50)}{200,000}$$

$$= 1.75$$

This level of DOL means that if sales increase by 1 percent, EBIT will increase by 1.75 percent; if sales increase by 10 percent, EBIT will increase by 17.5 percent; if sales increase by 15 percent, EBIT will increase by 26.25 percent (15% × 1.75).

How to Calculate Degree of Financial Leverage

DFL is easier to calculate than DOL. DFL is simply a ratio of EBIT divided by EBIT minus fixed *financial* costs (usually simply interest expense).

$$\text{DFL} = \frac{\text{EBIT}}{\text{EBIT-Interest}}$$

$$= \frac{200,000}{200,000 - 20,000}$$

$$= 1.11$$

In other words, if EBIT increases by 10 percent, net income will increase by 11.1 percent. (10% × 1.11). If EBIT decreases by 15 percent, net income will decrease by 16.65 percent.

How to Calculate Degree of Combined Leverage

The easiest way to calculate DCL simply to multiply DOL. times DFL.

$$DCL = DOL \times DFL$$
$$= 1.75 \times 1.11$$
$$= 1.94$$

Once you have determined the DCL for a company or process, it can be used to "back into" the needed sales target to produce any desired increase in profits.

Assume the DCL is 2.00. If you want to increase net income by 10 percent, a sales increase of 5 percent will be needed. If DCL is 5.00, a sales increase of only 2 percent will produce the desired increase in profits.

Leverage Analysis Based on Dollars of Sales

In the event you don't have information on actual units produced and sold with a given cost structure, you may need to calculate leverage on the basis of dollar sales. If so, the assumptions about constant prices and product mix become particularly important. Over the short run and over a narrow range of assumed output and sales levels, such assumptions may be reasonable.

Degree of Operating Leverage

The degree of operating leverage is simply total dollar contribution (rather than contribution per unit) divided by EBIT. Total dollar contribution is equal to total sales minus total variable costs.

	# 1	# 2
Sales	$1,000,0000	$1,000,000
Total variable costs:		
Materials & factory overhead	200,000	200,000
Labor	500,000	0
Total contribution	300,000	800,000

	#1	#2
Fixed operating:		
Depreciation	0	500,000
EBIT	300,000	300,000
Interest	188,000	0

$$\text{D.O.L.} = \frac{\text{Sales-Variable Costs}}{\text{EBIT}}$$

$$\begin{array}{cc}
\text{Company \# 1} & \text{Company \# 2} \\
= \dfrac{\$1,000,000 - 700,000}{300,000} & \dfrac{\$1,000,000 - 200,000}{300,000} \\
\\
= \quad 1.00 & 2.67
\end{array}$$

Degree of Financial Leverage

The degree of financial leverage is still EBIT divided by EBIT minus interest expense (note that this is the same as earnings before taxes).

$$\text{DFL} = \frac{\text{EBIT}}{\text{EBIT-Interest}}$$

$$\begin{array}{cc}
\text{Company \# 1} & \text{Company \# 2} \\
= \dfrac{300,000}{300,000 - 188,000} & \dfrac{300,000}{300,000 - 0} \\
\\
= \quad 2.67 & 1.00
\end{array}$$

Degree of Combined Leverage

The degree of combined leverage is still equal to (DOL) × (DFL). Alternatively, we can see that it is equal to total contribution divided by EBIT minus interest.

$$\text{DCL} = (\text{DOL}) \times (\text{DFL})$$

$$\begin{array}{cc}
\text{Company \# 1} & \text{Company \# 2} \\
= (1.00 \times 2.67) & (2.67 \times 1.00) \\
= \quad 2.67 & 2.67
\end{array}$$

## 17

Pro Forma Statements

EXECUTIVE SUMMARY

Pro forma statements are hypothetical (projected) income statements and balance sheets. They are used in order to anticipate the financial consequences of alternative courses of action. They are used, for example, in investment analysis and in developing financing plans. Pro forma statements are also developed in order to investigate the financial consequences of corporate plans.

Strengths:

- May provide good estimates of short-run performance
- Permit estimates of financing requirements
- Internally consistent (e.g. pro forma income statement ties into pro forma balance sheet)
- Bring together assumptions and forecasts of all major functions

- Help anticipate change by forcing management's attention on future
- Show probable impacts of major decision before decision is made
- Help formulate targets for profits and asset management and enable performance assessment
- Through use of ratios, pro formas can be related to prior management performance
- Data requirements can be minor (such as current year's data) and easily collected

Limitations:

- Many assumptions may be hidden and prove to be inaccurate
- You may be held too rigidly (by lenders) to meeting pro forma targets even though circumstances have changed
- May lead to false sense of certainty and precision because they are internally consistent
- Beyond one or two years may have little meaning

Pro Forma Income Statements

Pro forma income statements employ the same cost distinction as do break-even and leverage analyses: variable costs and fixed costs. However, while in break-even and leverage analyses we broke up the income statement into fixed and variable cost categories, in developing pro forma income statements we need to reconstitute these elements into their proper representation.

Given the classification of costs developed in Chapter 16, all we need is some assumed (or projected) level of sales. Of course, we are assuming that the cost characteristics we have developed will continue for the sales level used.

Pro forma income statements provide the same essential information as a leverage analysis, but they are more detailed and employ the format as it would actually appear in financial reports.

Pro forma statements are essential for purposes of investment analysis because they project the expected profits and cash flows over the investment's life. Where little prior experience with the proposed investment exists, pro forma statements spell out the assumptions incorporated in the profit projections.

Based on the same assumptions as break-even and leverage analyses, pro forma income statements are susceptible to the same weaknesses in assumed relationships.

How to Construct a Pro Forma Income Statement

Estimated from Chapter 15 we have the following relationships:

Variable Costs (% Sales)	
Cost of goods sold	60%
Selling (variable portion)	3%
Gen'l & administrative (variable portion)	2%
Fixed Costs	
Selling (fixed portion)	$20,000
Gen'l & admin. (fixed portion)	80,000
Depreciation	50,000
Interest	20,000

These estimates are based on the existing sales level of $1,000,000, and they are assumed to continue at a higher sales level. A pro forma income statement reflecting a sales level 15 percent higher is shown below:

Pro Forma Income Statement for the year ending December 31, 19X3

Sales ($1,000,000 plus 15%)		$1,150,000
Cost of goods sold (60% of sales)		690,000
Gross profit		460,000
Operating expenses:		
Selling ($20,000 plus 3% sales)	54,500	
Gen'l & admin. ($80,000 plus		
2% of sales)	103,000	
Depreciation	50,000	207,500
Operating Profit		252,500
Nonoperating expenses:		
Interest		20,000

Earnings before taxes	232,500
Taxes (50%)	116,250
Net income	116,250

Sales

Assume that sales growth in 19X3 is an increase 15 percent over 19X2. Then total sales will be:

$$\$1,000,000 \text{ plus } 15\% = \$1,150,000$$

Cost of Goods Sold

Cost of goods sold is estimated to be 60 percent of sales. Therefore, at the new level of sales, cost of goods sold will be $690,000.

$$\$1,150,000 \times 60\% = \$690,000$$

Gross Profit

Gross profit is equal to sales minus cost of goods sold, or, $460,000.

$$\text{Gross Profit} = \text{Sales minus Cost of goods sold}$$
$$= \$1,150,000 - 690,000$$
$$= \$460,000$$

Operating Expenses

Operating expenses is made up of selling, general and administrative, and depreciation expenses.

Selling expense is partly fixed and partly variable. The variable portion (3 percent of sales), will amount to $34,500 in 19X3:

$$\text{Variable portion} = 3\% \times \$1,150,000$$
$$= \$34,500$$

The fixed portion of selling expense is not expected to increase with the higher sales volume, it will remain at $20,000.

Total Selling Expense = variable portion + fixed portion
= $34,500 + $20,000
= $54,500

General and administrative expenses contain a variable portion (2 percent of sales) plus a fixed portion ($80,000). Thus, in 19X3, total general and administrative expenses will be $103,000.

Variable portion (2% sales) = 2% × $1,150,000
= $23,000
Fixed portion   = $80,000
TOTAL $103,000

Depreciation expense is completely fixed relative to sales. Thus, in 19X3 it is expected to remain at $50,000.
Total operating expenses are thus expected to be $207,500.

Operating Profit (EBIT)

Operating profit is equal to gross profit minus all operating expenses. Thus, in 19X3, operating profit is expected to be $252,500.

Operating profit = Gross profit minus operating expenses
= $460,000 − $207,500
= $252,500

Interest

I have treated interest expense as completely fixed relative to sales and thus totaling $20,000 in 19X3.

Earnings Before Taxes

Earnings before taxes are equal to operating profit less nonoperating expenses (in this case, interest expense). In 19X3, this will be $232,500.

Earnings before taxes = Operating profit minus
nonoperating expenses
= $252,500 − $20,000
= $232,500

Taxes

Taxes are 50 percent of earnings before taxes. Thus, in 19X3, taxes will be $116,250.

$$\text{Taxes} = (\$232,500) \times 50\%$$
$$= \$116,250$$

Net Income

Net income is equal to earnings before taxes minus taxes, or $116,250.

$$\text{Net Income} = \text{earnings before taxes less taxes}$$
$$= \$232,500 - \$116,250$$
$$= \$116,250$$

The Full Statement

The full statement requires only putting together each of the individual estimates into the proper format. This is shown on pages 134–135.

Pro Forma Balance Sheet

The pro forma balance sheet is a hypothetical estimate of the company's financial position at some assumed level of sales. Most of the items on the balance sheet can be estimated through the use of ratios. For example, if accounts receivable average about fifty days of sales outstanding and this is expected to continue, knowing the anticipated sales can yield good estimates of the pro forma accounts receivable.

At a hypothetical sales level of $2,000,000, what can we expect accounts receivable to total, assuming the average collection period (ACP) stays at fifty days? Remember that

$$\text{ACP} = \frac{\text{Accounts receivable}}{\text{Total sales}/360 \text{ days}}$$

Therefore,

$$\text{Accounts receivable} = \text{ACP} \times \text{Total sales}/360$$
$$= 50 \text{ days} \times 2,000,000/360$$
$$= \$277,780$$

However, certain balance sheet items are not related to sales in any direct way. For example, the level of plant and equipment from one year to the next is not likely to change in response to sales. Over a period of years, an average relationship between fixed assets and sales will emerge, but this average is unlikely to be reliable on a year-to-year basis.

Preparation of pro forma balance sheets thus involves (1) an understanding of certain asset/sales relationships, (2) identification of rigidities in the usage of assets, and (3) knowledge of relatively transient events that impact on the balance sheet accounts (such as miscellaneous current assets or liabilities).

As a forecast and planning document, the pro forma balance sheet usually tries to highlight implications of projected sales on the cash balance and/or external funds requirements.

How to Construct a Pro Forma Balance Sheet

The first thing to identify is the purpose of the pro forma. Are you trying to figure out how much additional financing you will need at a higher sales level? Are you trying to determine the impact of altered credit policy on financial requirements? Let's assume that you are concerned with the impact on the level of needed bank borrowings that will result from a 15 percent increase in sales volume. If you are concerned with the impact on bank borrowings, you need to estimate all other items on the balance sheet *except* bank borrowings. Bank borrowings will therefore become the "plug" figure, or the amount that brings the balance sheet into balance. Otherwise, the development of a pro forma balance sheet is simply a matter of "filling in the blanks."

Filling in the blanks involves using a considerable amount of judgment and making assumptions that could be second-guessed. Yet what we are trying to derive is an estimate rather than the "true" figures. It is absolutely essential, however, that whatever estimates are incorporated in the pro forma balance sheet be consistent with *any other projected statements, such as the pro forma income statement* estimated earlier or a projected cash budget, if any.

Pro Forma Balance Sheet as of 12/31/X3

Cash	_____	Accounts payable	_____
Accounts receivable	_____	Bank loans	_____
Inventory	_____	Current liab.	_____
Current assets	_____	Long-term debt	_____

Gross fixed assets	_____	Deferred income tax	_____
Less acc. deprec.	_____	Total liabilities	_____
Net fixed assets	_____	Shareholders' equity	
		Common Stock	_____
TOTAL ASSETS	_____	Retained earnings	_____
		TOTAL LIABILITIES AND SHAREHOLDERS' EQ.	_____

In estimating, let us assume that sales are expected to grow by 15 percent from the 19X2 level and that the same general financial ratios that existed in 19X2 will continue into 19X3.

Estimating Cash

There is no obvious way of determining the projected level of cash. We might simply assume some minimum level as established by the company management or we might assume that it is roughly proportional to the level of sales, say just about 1 percent of sales (using the 19X2 figures). At a level of 1 percent of sales, cash should be roughly $12,000.

$$\text{Cash} = 1\% \times \text{Sales}$$
$$= .01 \times \$1,150,000$$
$$= \$11,500$$

Estimating Accounts Receivable

Remembering that the average collection period is 50.4 days. The formula for ACP is:

$$\text{ACP} = \frac{\text{Accounts receivable}}{\text{Sales/day}}$$

If ACP stays at 50.4, the new sales level of $1,150,000 equals $3,194/day, so accounts receivable will be:

$$\text{ACP} \times \text{Sales/day} = \text{Accounts receivable}$$
$$50.4 \times \$3,194.4 = \$161,000$$

Estimating Inventory

Since we are assuming the same performance as in 19X2, inventory turnover is 6.0 times, based on cost of goods sold. Remember that cost of goods sold is 60 percent of sales (this is also consistent with the pro forma income statement). At the new sales level of $1,150,000, cost of goods sold will be $690,000 and inventory will be $175,000.

$$\frac{\text{Cost of goods sold}}{\text{Inventory}} = \text{Inventory turnover}$$

and, therefore,

$$\frac{\text{Cost of goods sold}}{\text{Inventory turnover}} = \text{Inventory amount (\$)}$$

$$\frac{\$690,000}{6.0} = \$115,000$$

Estimating Net Fixed Assets

In 19X2, gross fixed assets increased by $50,000. Unless we have better information, it might be reasonable to assume a similar increase in 19X3. Accumulated depreciation will increase by $50,000 (this is consistent with the depreciation charged off in the pro forma income statement). Net fixed assets will be unchanged at $250,000 since the change in gross fixed assets is exactly offset by the increase in accumulated depreciation.

	19X2	19X3
Gross fixed assets	$400,000	$450,000
Less acc. depreciation	− 150,000	− 200,000
Net fixed assets	$250,000	$250,000

Combining the Asset Estimates

We have now estimated all the major asset accounts.

Cash		12
Accounts receivable		161
Inventory		115
Current assets		288
Gross fixed assets	$450	
Less acc. deprec.	200	
Net fixed assets		250
Total assets		$538

Estimating Accounts Payable

We have insufficient information to calculate accounts payable, but in the absence of better data we might assume that they will maintain the relationship they had to sales in 19X2.

$$\text{Accounts payable (\% of Sales)} = \frac{\text{Accounts payable}}{\text{Sales}}$$

$$\text{Accounts payable (19X2)} = \frac{\$75,000}{\$1,000,000}$$

$$= .075$$

Using the 19X2 relationship, accounts payable in 19X3 would be about $86,000.

$$\text{Accounts Payable (19X3)} = .075 \times \$1,150,000$$
$$= \$86,250$$

Estimating Bank Loans

Since bank loans will be our "plug" figure, we will reserve this estimate for the last.

Estimating Long-Term Debt

In 19X2 long-term debt was reduced by $40,000. Since there are no current maturities of long-term debt shown on the 19X2 balance sheet, it is possible that the level of long-term debt is not going to be reduced further in 19X3. If so, it will stay at the 19X2 level of $150,000.

Estimating Deferred Income Taxes

Deferred income taxes usually increase as the company expands. To be conservative, let's assume there is no increase over the 19X2 level of $50,000.

Estimating Common Stock

This figure increases with new common stock issues. Since we have no reason to expect the company to issue more stock in 19X3, the 19X3 figure will be the same as in 19X2, or $75,000.

Estimating Retained Earnings

The retained earnings account will increase with new net income less any dividends paid out. Remember that in 19X2 Tasbem paid out 44 percent of its net income. If we assume the same for 19X3, dividends will be:

$$\text{Dividends (19X3)} = .44 \times \$116,250 \text{ (from pro forma I/S)}$$
$$= \$51,150$$

A dividend of $51,150 will leave about $65,000 in new retained earnings. The 19X3 retained earnings figure will be:

Retained earnings 19X2	$100,000
Plus new retained earnings	65,100
Retained earnings 19X3	$165,100

Combining Estimates

We now have estimates for all items except, of course, bank loans (the "plug" figure). Let's see what we have.

Cash	12	Accounts payable	86
Accounts receivable	161	Bank loans	?
Inventory	115	Current liabilities:	
Current assets	288	Long-term debt	150
Gross fixed assets	450	Deferred income taxes	50
Less acc. deprec.	200	Shareholders' equity:	
Net fixed assets	250	Common stock	75
Total assets	538	Retained earnings	165
		Total (except bank loans)	$526
		Bank loan required	12
		Total Liabilities & S.E.	538

As the pro forma balance sheet reveals, bank loans totaling $12,000 are implied by the higher sales growth. Since Tasbem currently is borrowing $50,000, the pro forma indicates that much of the bank debt can be repaid by the end of 19X3. In fact, based on the estimates incorporated, $38,000 of current bank borrowings will be unneeded by year end 19X3.

## 18

Financial Limits to Growth

EXECUTIVE SUMMARY

Given a few strategic assumptions about a firm's operating characteristics and financial policies, it is possible to estimate the growth potential in sales from year to year and over a period of several years. If a company attempts to grow faster than its potential, it will run into trouble, forcing a violation of financial policies. Most small, rapidly growing companies fail to foresee this difficulty and ultimately find themselves in a severe liquidity crisis. Often the only answer to the severe liquidity problem is a cutback of growth plans.

The simple formula presented in this chapter can prove very useful in estimating the growth potential of a company, given four assumptions (or estimates):

- Attainable net profit margin on sales
- Expected asset/sales ratio

- Percentage of annual earnings retained
- Total debt/equity ratio

There is also an implicit assumption that the company will not issue additional common stock shares. This is a realistic assumption for smaller companies in particular, but also for large companies, which generally do not routinely rely on common stock issues as a form of financing.

Strengths:

- Easy to calculate
- Easy to use
- Good approximation over short periods
- Focuses on strategic financial variables
- Permits sensitivity analysis of operating and policy variables

Limitations:

- Strategic financial variables may change on short notice

Just as there are capacity constraints on a company's output growth, and just as there are market share constraints on sales growth opportunities, so too are there financial limitations to sales expansion. If a company is opposed to sales of new common stock, these financial limits can be estimated by combining four simple ratios into one formula:

$$G = \frac{(M \times R \times L)}{A-(M \times R \times L)}$$

G = maximum sustainable growth rate in assets and sales
M = profit margin on sales
R = Percentage of annual earnings retained
L = Debt/equity ratio plus 1.0
A = Assets/sales ratio

A

As a company's sales grow, it needs more assets to support the sales growth. The asset/sales ratio is important because it lets us estimate quickly the level of assets required at every given sales level.

An asset/sales ratio of 1.0 means that $1 of assets is needed to support $1 of sales. An asset/sales ratio of .5 means that, on the average, 50 cents of investment is needed to support $1 of sales.

In order to pay for the assets required by the expanded sales volume, the company must raise the funds. There are two basic sources of funds: shareholders' investment (equity) and debt (all liabilities, including trade credit, bank loans, and long-term debt). The ratios M, R and L represent these sources.

M

M represents the profit margin on sales.

R

Equity is raised in two ways: (1) a sale of common stock by the company and (2) reinvestment of profits earned. Since companies are extremely reluctant to issue common stock (for reasons discussed later), the source of equity funds from one year to the next for company is usually restricted to retained earnings. The ratio R represents the percentage of total net income that a company retains (reinvests).

If a company's net profits are $100 and it pays out $40 in dividends, retained earnings will increase by $60 and its *retention rate* (R) is 60 percent.

L

The amount of debt a company can tap depends on the level of its equity. For example, a firm that can get $2 of debt for each $1 of equity has a debt/equity ratio of 2.0 and an L of 3.0.

If a company increases its equity (through an increase in retained earnings) by $50, a debt/equity ratio of 2.0 will imply borrowing capacity of $100 more.

Using the Formula

Assume that you know the following information about a company:

- Sales are $1,000
- Net profits are $100

- Dividends paid are $50
- Total assets are $1,000
- Total liabilities are $500
- Total shareholders' equity is $500

With these *six* items, you can estimate the company's financial growth potential.

$$\text{M: } \frac{\text{Net income}}{\text{Sales}} = \frac{\$100}{\$1,000} = .10$$

$$\text{R: } \frac{\text{Net income} - \text{Dividends}}{\text{Net income}} = \frac{\$100 - \$50}{\$100} = .50$$

$$\text{L: } \frac{D}{E} + 1 = \frac{\text{Total liabilities}}{\text{Shareholders' equity}} + 1.0 = \frac{500}{500} + 1.0 = 2.0$$

$$\text{A: } \frac{\text{Assets}}{\text{Sales}} = \frac{\$1,000}{\$1,000} = 1.0$$

Figure 18.1 shows how these variables are combined to estimate the firm's growth potential.

Figure 18.1

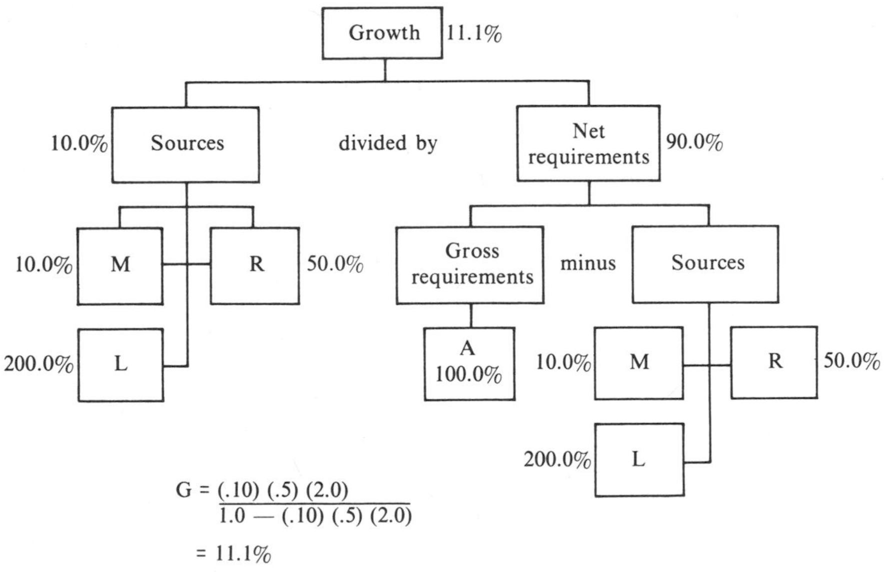

$$G = \frac{(.10)\,(.5)\,(2.0)}{1.0 - (.10)\,(.5)\,(2.0)}$$

$$= 11.1\%$$

Interpretation

Given the characteristics of the company, sales can grow at the rate of 11.1 percent per year indefinitely. If the company attempts to grow at a faster rate, given these financial characteristics, the company will experience diminishing liquidity, until suddenly activities will freeze up as cash evaporates.

Conversely, if the company grows at a slower rate, say 5 percent, excess liquidity will build up, causing the asset/sales ratio to rise.

How and Why the Freeze-up Occurs

Let's see how a company can freeze up financially if it tries to maintain its financial performance and policies while trying to grow faster than its sustainable rate.

Asset Requirements

With a growth rate of 15 percent, sales volume will be $1,150, an increase of $150. Since the asset/sales ratio is 1.0, assets will also have to expand by $150. How will these assets be paid for?

Profits

With a profit margin of 10 percent, net income will be $115. However, the dividend payout rate is 50 percent, so only $57.50 will be kept in the company.

$$\text{Profits} = (.10) \times \$1150.00$$
$$= \$115$$
$$\text{Retained earnings increase} = (.50) \times \$115$$
$$= \$57.50$$

New Debt

The company's debt/equity ratio is 1.0, so additional borrowings of $57.50 will be possible.

$$\text{New debt} = (1.0) \times \$57.50$$
$$= \$57.50$$

Cash Shortage

A cash shortage is clearly inevitable, because the company needs $150 for new assets. But only $57.50 (equity) plus $57.50 (new debt) or $115 will be available.

Since the assets can't be purchased sales will not be generated, and the 15 percent growth will not be possible.

The "Right" Path

Let's see what happens if the company pursues its "proper" growth rate of 11.1 percent.

- Sales increase by 11.1 percent or $111.10
- Assets increase by $111.10

How will the assets be paid for?

- net income will be 10 percent of $1111.00, or $111.10, of which half will be kept in the company: $55.55.
- Debt will increase by the amount of the increase in equity, or $55.55

Total sources of funds will increase by $111.10, enough to pay for the added asset requirements.

How to Increase Your Growth Potential

There are surprisingly few things company management can do to raise its financial growth potential. With the exception of a possible common stock issue (to increase equity and raise more debt), a company is limited to the four variables described above.

Raise the Debt/Equity Ratio

If the company increases its target ratio of debt to equity, a faster rate of growth is possible, although financial risk will obviously increase. If the debt/equity rate rises to 2.0 from its current level of 1.0, the value of L will be 3.0. If no other variables change, the new growth potential is:

$$G = \frac{(.10) \times (.5) \times (3.0)}{1.0 - (.10) \times (.5) \times (3.0)}$$
$$= .18$$

Raise the Earnings Retention Rate

An increase in the earnings retention rate means that more profits will be kept in the company. These additional retentions will also support more debt. Of course, a higher retention rate means less in dividends per dollar of earnings to shareholders.

If the company decided to pay *no* dividends but otherwise did not alter its original financial characteristics, the growth potential for the company will rise to:

$$G = \frac{(.10) \times (1.0) \times (2.0)}{1.0 - (.10) \times (1.0) \times (2.0)}$$

$$= .25$$

or 25 percent per year.

Other Choices: A or M

A distinctive feature of the options just discussed is that they can be changed relatively easily because they represent financial *policies*. As such, management has much (though not total) discretion over what they will be (for example, the retention rate could be set anywhere between zero and 100 percent. The debt/equity rate could be set between zero and the maximum allowed by lenders). Management options, however, with respect to either the profit margin on sales or the asset/sales ratio (performance ratios) is severely limited by the type of business the company is in.

## 19

Cash Budgets

EXECUTIVE SUMMARY

The cash budget is the most vital financial document in the company, because it keeps track of the cash into and out of the company's bank account. The cash budget is used as a planning document as well as a mechanism for controlling operations.

Strengths:

- Can be useful in planning and controlling operations
- Can be used to anticipate emerging funds needs and surplus
- Can be used to establish performance targets and measure performance
- Can be used to integrate and coordinate activities
- Incorporates assumptions and forecasts of all functional managers

Limitations

- Can lock companies into inflexible targets
- May conceal many arguable assumptions
- May inhibit responsiveness to change

The cash budget is your most vital financial document. Unlike the income statement and balance sheet, the cash budget focuses directly on the factor of major importance to company survival: cash. Therefore, while the cash budget will not directly reveal either profitability or financial condition, it does reflect the implications of these factors for the flows of cash into, around, and through the company. In short, the cash budget reveals the liquidity position of the company.

What Is "Cash"?

You know what cash is, of course, but on the balance sheet cash does not simply refer to the greenbacks in the petty cash fund. Cash is the money in the petty cash fund as well as the money on deposit at the banks.

Often cash and "near cash" securities are lumped together in the cash shown on the balance sheet. The "near cash" items are short-term investments called marketable securities.

Cash Budget as a Management Tool

As a forecasting document, the cash budget combines projections of sales and production activities as well as other planned inflows and outflows over a period of time that may extend over days, weeks, months, or even years. The idea is to project the impacts of these flows on the cash balance of the company. For example, the cash budget could reveal an impending cash shortage, when the shortage will occur, and how it should be met (e.g. by borrowing or liquidation of short-term investments).

Once the impacts on cash are identified, measured, and timed, you can prepare a plan of action to meet expected shortages or to handle expected cash excesses.

If the cash budget projects shortages of $10, $15, and $20 during the first three months of the forecast period, you know that you will have to arrange cash infusions for those periods in addition to the inflows you are currently expecting—with total infusions of $45 by the end of the third month. You might plan to liquidate marketable securities investments, if possible, to meet the requirements. Or you might now request a standby line of credit from the bank to cover that amount or more.

If these alternatives are not possible or desirable, then you will have to take steps to reduce scheduled cash outflows (maybe not paying bills as planned) or to increase cash inflows (maybe requesting more prompt payments from customers).

On the other hand, if you anticipate a substantial buildup of excess cash, you should plan for its productive redeployment.

What the Cash Budget Looks Like

There are many stylistic variations in practice, but the cash budget consists of three principal parts:

Part I: Cash inflows
Part II: Cash outflows
Part III: Financing

Table 19.1 presents an example of a cash budget for the Joy Company covering the period January through March.

Part I: Cash Inflows

Part I identifies the source, amount, and timing of all anticipated cash inflows in each of the periods under consideration. A period may range from days to months or years.

Cash is mainly generated from sales: cash sales and collections from previous sales made on credit. If only a small percentage of sales are made for cash, the bulk of these cash inflows will represent collections of accounts receivable, as customers pay. Other cash inflows for a period may reflect such things as cash received from the sale of fixed assets (not a common occurrence) or interest income earned. It does not make any difference whether cash is generated by an "income statement" transaction, such as sales, or by a "balance sheet" transac-

TABLE 19.1. Joy Company Cash Budget

	JANUARY	FEBRUARY	MARCH
PART I. Inflows			
Collections	$12,000	$21,000	$31,000
Part II. Outflows			
Purchases	14,000	15,000	20,000
Wages & salaries	1,500	2,000	2,500
Rent	500	500	500
Miscellany	100	100	100
Taxes		10,500	
Total outflows	16,100	28,100	23,100
PART III. Financing			
Net inflow (out)	(4,100)	(7,100)	7,900
Cumulative inflow (out)	(4,100)	(11,200)	(3,300)
Beginning cash 10,000			
Less minimum 8,000			
Available 2,000	2,000	2,000	2,000
Net excess (borrowing)	(2,100)	(9,200)	(1,300)

tion, such as a sale of assets. If it is a cash inflow, it should show up in Part I of the cash budget.

Part II: Cash Outflows

Part II of the cash budget is concerned with identifying for each period all cash outflows anticipated for whatever use. For example, if you are planning a capital expenditure, will have to make tax payments, or are scheduled to pay dividends, these disbursements will have to be included.

In addition, cash outflows in support of production and merchandising activities will be needed for materials, labor, rent, lease payments, utilities, and so on. If you get credit from suppliers, the materials payments will reflect payments for purchases in some prior period (in other words, payment of accounts payable).

Part III: Financing

Part III of the cash budget brings together cash inflows and outflows in each period and shows their net impacts on the cash position and financing requirments of the company each period.

Cash "Excess," "Shortage," and "Minimum"

"Minimum" cash is the lowest level of cash that the company wants to keep on deposit to meet transaction requirements safely. The minimum cash balance includes not only enough cash to meet expected requirements but also a safety "buffer." Excess cash is cash above the desired minimum. A cash shortage is cash below the desired minimum.

If the cash budget should show excesses rather than shortages in the first three months of $10, $15, and $25, respectively, you should repay short-term borrowings or plan for the safe reinvestment of such cash.

Cash Budget as a Control Document

The cash budget can also be an important control document. Once formulated, the projections should become targets. Anticipated cash requirements can be compared with actual usage. Large deviations in one direction or another signal areas to investigate.

The preparation and implementation of the cash budget can be used to get agreement and cooperation throughout the company on company plans. If the available cash will not allow all proposed and desired activities to be undertaken, the cash budget can be used to force decisions and agreements as to which activities should have priority.

Since a shortage of cash in one period can be offset by surpluses of cash in other periods, the cumulative effect of inflows and outflows is of most importance.

You expect a cash shortage in the second month equal to $25, but in the first month you will have an excess of $40. No borrowings will be needed in either period, since the excess in month 1 will more than adequately offset the shortage in the second month. On a cumulative basis, you have an excess of $40 in the first month and an excess of $15 as of the end of the second month.

Month	1	2
Cash excess (shortage)	$40	($25)
Cumulative cash excess (shortage)	$40	$15

## PART FOUR

Working Asset Management

This part focuses on ways to determine whether investment in working assets is as productive as possible and describes ways in which working assets can be made more productive. This part includes the following chapters:

20. Cash Management
21. Accounts Receivable Management
22. Inventory Management

Working Assets and ROI

Working assets refer to the current assets held by the company. These assets, like all others, must be financed, and thus they represent investment funds. Excessive working capital can hurt ROI by raising the amount of investment employed relative to the profits generated.

Let's say companies A and B are identical in all respects except that A has much more working capital then B does.

	A	B
Sales	$10,000,000	$10,000,000
Net income	1,000,000	1,000,000
Current assets	3,000,000	1,000,000
Fixed assets	7,000,000	7,000,000
Total assets	$10,000,000	$8,000,000

$$\text{ROI} \quad \frac{1,000,000}{10,000,000} = 10\% \qquad \frac{1,000,000}{8,000,000} = 12.5\%$$

A's performance has been hurt by its greater investment in current assets.

Working Capital Uses

Working capital investments are made to support day-to-day operations and sales activities. These include:

- The amount of cash and marketable securities you have
- The amount of credit you extend
- The amounts and types of inventories you have

Normal Working Capital Investment

The proportions of total assets represented by working capital and the relationship of working capital to sales vary significantly from one type of business to another. For mining companies current assets may average 30 percent of total assets. For retail companies, the average is over 60 percent, and for wholesalers the average is over 70 percent.

The level of working capital needed by a company is closely tied to sales and production activities. For example, as sales increases, more credit is extended to customers, more finished goods inventory is needed on hand, more work-in-process is needed to meet future orders, and more raw materials inventory is needed to support the increased production requirements. As production and purchase activities increase, more cash for operating requirements is also needed.

The long-run trend of sales is usually upward, even though there may be deviations from year to year around the trend line. On the accompanying graph, for example, in 19X2 sales were down, but this was a temporary decline. Working capital requirements dropped, but this was temporary as well.

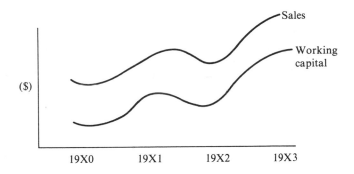

Working Capital Management

As working capital needs rise and fall, it is important to manage actual levels of investment to make sure they reflect existing needs and profit potential.

The objective of working capital management is to make sure that each type of working capital investment is productive in (1) generating income for the business, (2) reducing the amount of investment needed to support sales and production, or (3) both.

Since working capital requirements are volatile, you need to have highly flexible financing sources to absorb the rapid changes in investment needed. The primary sources of financing flexibility are trade credit and bank debt. These and other sources of financing are discussed in Part VI, "Managing the Cost of Funds."

## 20

Cash Management

EXECUTIVE SUMMARY

Cash and near-cash assets are your primary resources for financial mobility. This mobility has a cost: It reduces overall ROI performance. Excessive cash balances unnecessarily weaken ROI performance.

You should check the levels of cash and marketable securities under your control to see if they are "reasonable." You can do this by calculating the ratio of cash and marketable securities as a percentage of sales. If this ratio is much higher than the industry norm, investigate why. One thing to check is the efficiency of cash collection procedures. Maybe a lot of the "cash" is uncollected funds, which represents checks that have been deposited but not "cleared" at the bank. Another thing to check is whether you are passing up opportunities safely to exploit the float available to you.

Finally, once you have determined the appropriate overall level of cash and marketable securities to hold, make sure that these balances work as hard as possible.

Strengths:

- Helps ROI
- May not be hard to implement
- Techniques well understood by most large banks

Limitations:

- Mistakes can be embarrassing and costly
- Cash management programs may be costly
- May take up too much management time
- Overly aggressive cash management may hurt "goodwill" with banks, suppliers, and customers

---

The objective of cash management is to contribute to overall ROI while providing sufficient liquidity to meet planned and unexpected requirements.

Safety in Cash Management

The most crucial requirement of cash management is to have sufficient cash to meet cash needs. The best guide to cash requirements is the cash budget: It tells you when you will need cash and how much cash you will need.

Beyond transactions requirements, companies include a buffer or "reserve" in the cash account in the event actual cash requirements exceed estimates.

Cash Management and ROI

It's always nice to have a lot of cash, but it has a cost. The "cost" of holding a lot of cash is the lower ROI you will earn. For example, consider companies A and B. They are identical in every respect, except that A has a lot more cash, which ties up more total investment. Notice that because of its greater cash A's return on investment is only 20 percent, as against B's 22 percent return.

Cash Management

		A		B
Net income		200		200
Assets				
Cash	100		10	
A/R	400		400	
Inventory	200		200	
	700		610	
Net fixed assets	300		300	
Total assets	1000		910	
ROI		20%		22%

Increasing Overall ROI

There are two ways in which effective cash management can contribute to overall improvement in ROI:

1. Increase the profit contributions of "cash"
2. Decrease the amount of investment tied up in the cash account

Increasing Returns: Marketable Securities

Your cash budget will often reveal periods of time in which a temporary excess of cash will develop. Except for special accounts, cash on deposit at banks does not earn income—it has zero ROI. So excess cash should first be used to repay any existing short-term debt. If there is no outstanding short-term debt, the temporary cash excess should be invested in marketable securities.

Marketable securities are short-term investments that produce interest income. They are the closest thing to cash you can invest in.

Marketable securities are very low risk, can be sold for cash in an instant, and provide a "yield" or return on investment. Some marketable securities have investment "lives" as short as one day.

Liquidity is crucial, since we have assumed that the cash excess is temporary. As cash requirements begin to build again, it will be necessary to liquidate investments in marketable securities and convert the investment into cash.

In addition to temporary cash excesses, most if not all the "safety buffer" cash can be invested in marketable securities.

Three Ways to Make Cash More Productive

There are three ways to improve the ROI productivity of cash

1. Make sure that cash is collected as quickly as possible.
2. Improve the cash forecasting system in order to reduce the required safety buffer and improve opportunities to play the float.
3. "Play the float" by minimizing the idle time of bank cash.

Accelerate Collections

Before considering specific techniques for accelerating cash inflows, imagine what the "unaccelerated" cash collection procedure might be. Figure 20.1 provides an example intended to illustrate all the possible sources of delay in collecting checks. (Typically, few companies would be guilty of all of these "sins.")

In the "natural" course of business payments, the customer (A) purchases goods or services from the company (B) and pays with a check. Following receipt of A's check B might then process the check internally, perhaps matching the check with the customer invoice, and so on. After its internal processing of A's check, B sends the check to its own bank (C). If the deposit is mailed, of course, further delay occurs. When bank C receives the check deposit it then must send it to A's bank (D) for clearance ("collection"). This mail time presents further delay in getting cash to corporation B. When bank D clears A's check it reduces A's bank balance, notifies A that the check has been cleared,

Figure 20.1   Possible Delays in a Check Collection System

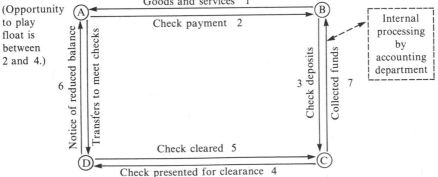

and also informs (via mail) bank C that the funds have been collected. Bank C then informs company B that its collected balance has increased.

For a large corporation, with customers spread out around the country, mailing delays alone can constitute substantial tying up of funds. These delays are called "float." When the delays slow down your receipt of cash, that is "negative float." When the delays give you longer use of cash (in other words, the people you pay have to wait longer), that is "positive float." You want to decrease negative float and increase positive float.

How to Decrease Negative Float:
Lock-Box Banking

The purpose of the lock-box system is to speed collection of checks (see Figure 20.2). The customer (A) is asked to send payments to a special post office box. Under the arrangement B's bank (C) sends messengers to the post office several times a day to collect all payments received. Bank C then separates the payments received from all other items (such as invoice copies) and sends the latter (along with a listing of checks) to corporation B. Bank C sends the checks received to the various customers' banks (e.g., bank D) for clearance. Bank D then processes the check and advises bank C that the check has been cleared. Bank C then advises B that its collected balance has increased.

"Playing the Float"

Playing the float means using the delays inherent in the check clearance system to your advantage. This float is the delay between when you write a check against your account and when the check finally gets presented against your account for payment.

You write a check on Monday, which you don't think will be presented for payment at your bank until Friday. You could deposit enough money to cover the check as of Monday and let it sit idly in the bank until Friday, or you could store the money in very short-term securities until Friday, liquidate your investment, and deposit the funds in your account.

Of course, if the check shows up at your bank on Thursday, it may bounce, unless you have made arrangements beforehand with the bank

Figure 20.2   Use of Lock-Box System to Decrease Negative Float

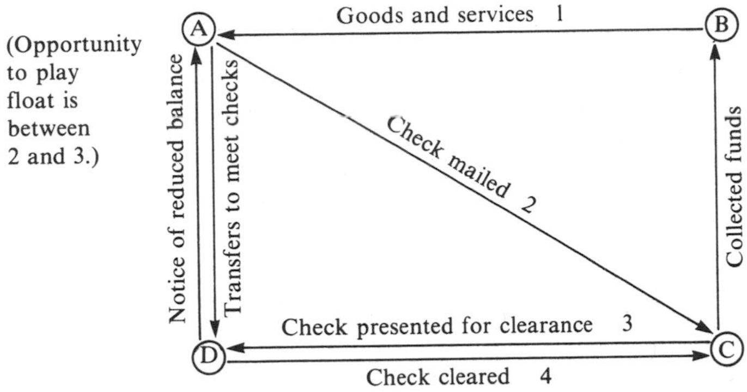

(Opportunity to play float is between 2 and 3.)

Goods and services 1

Check mailed 2

Check presented for clearance   3

Check cleared   4

Notice of reduced balance

Transfers to meet checks

Collected funds

to cover it. So you want to avoid playing the float too aggressively. But for every check that shows up earlier than expected, some other check will probably show up later than expected.

Increasing Positive Float: Delayed Disbursement

Mail times are the chief source of float, but float will also arise whenever the recipient of your check delays in mailing or depositing your check for collection. For example, if the check recipient waits until the check goes through the internal processing system before sending the check off for collection, all the delays involved contribute to the possible float.

Some companies more aggressively generate positive float by paying bills from accounts in the most distant banks and therefore maximizing mailing delays. In other words don't pay New York bills from New York bank accounts, pay them from accounts in California!

## 21

Accounts Receivable Management

EXECUTIVE SUMMARY

The amount of accounts receivable you have affects your overall ROI. You should check to see if your accounts receivable are excessive. A good way to check the reasonableness of accounts receivable is to compare your average collection period with the industry norm. If your average collection period is significantly higher, investigate the cause. Here are some things to look at:

- Is credit policy an important competitive weapon?
- Is credit monitoring effective for late payers?
- Are credit terms producing enough sales and profits to justify them?

Strengths:

- Can help ROI
- May not be hard to implement

- Easily modified, even reversed
- Can be used to evaluate many different changes in credit terms

Limitations:

- May incorrectly assume that sale increase is completely attributable to credit policy change
- May incorrectly assume that excess capacity is available
- May ignore competitors' reaction to change in credit policy.
- May not adequately assess credit risks and credit expenses

Accounts receivable represent the extension of credit to support sales. In many lines of business, the types and terms of credit granted by the firm are set by established competitive practices. As an investment, the accounts receivable should contribute to overall ROI.

Accounts Receivable Management and ROI

Excessive investment in accounts receivable can hurt ROI by tying up funds unnecessarily. Assume that companies A and B are identical in every way except that A has a lax credit policy which has resulted in $100 more tied up in accounts receivable than B does. As a result, A's ROI is only 22% compared to 25% for B.

Accounts Receivable

		A		B
Net income		200		200
Assets				
Cash	10		10	
A/R	400		300	
Inv.	200		200	
	610		510	
Net fixed assets	300		300	
Total assets	910		810	
ROI		22%		25%

How to Tell If Accounts Receivable Are Excessive

One good way to judge the extent of accounts receivable is to compare your average collection period with that of rivals or the industry average. If your average collection period is much higher than that for competitors or the industry norm, your accounts receivable are excessive.

Assume that you have credit sales of $720,000 and your average collection period is 50 days compared to 25 days for the industry overall. With these figures, your accounts receivable are $100,000, whereas they should be $50,000. This hurts ROI.

If your average collection period is excessive, it may be that you are not keeping tight control of late payers. One way to check this is to develop an aging schedule. The aging schedule shows how your accounts receivable are distributed with respect to being on time or late.

Accounts Receivable Aging Schedule

10%	less than 30 days (on time)
25%	30–40 days
30%	45–60 days
20%	60–90 days
15%	over 90 days

Failure to monitor late payments closely hurts ROI by tying up investment and also by weakening profits. The more overdue accounts become, the greater is the danger that they will be uncollectible and will have to be written off against profits.

If the aging schedule does not reveal excessive late accounts, your average collection period may be out of line simply because you are extending credit much more liberally than anybody else. Unless your more liberal credit policy is being translated into more competitive sales and greater profits than otherwise, it is advisable to rethink your credit program. In other words, you should attempt to estimate the ROI contribution of your more liberal credit policy. A technique for doing this is described in the next section.

Calculating Accounts Receivable ROI

When you liberalize credit or otherwise increase the amount of money tied up in accounts receivable, you expect to generate profits that you would not otherwise make. The ROI from accounts receivable investment is the ratio of profits resulting from the investment over the amount of investment. If this ROI is low, it will drag down overall ROI performance.

Assume that you can increase sales by $500,000 per year if you make credit terms easier. The investment in accounts receivable as a result of the easier credit will increase by $100,000. Assume that the increased sales will result in increased profits after taxes of $30,000. Your ROI on the change will be 30 percent.

Things to Watch Out For

The calculation of ROI above included some important assumptions, which should be recognized:

• It is assumed that the sales increased solely as a result of the change in credit terms. If sales would have increased anyway, then it is incorrect to attribute the greater profits to the accounts receivable investment.

• It is assumed that sufficient excess production capacity exists to produce the additional sales. If not, more fixed investment will be required, and this investment should be included when calculating ROI.

• It is assumed that the relationship between the increased sales and credit terms will continue. But if competitors respond with similar credit terms, sales and profits may drop while investment stays at the higher level. If this happens, of course, ROI may become zero or even negative on the credit terms.

• It is assumed that the increased credit risks in the easing of terms are properly recognized and evaluated.

• It is assumed that any increased administrative, clerical, credit check, and related expenses are taken into account in developing the increased profit estimate.

## 22

Inventory Management

EXECUTIVE SUMMARY

The inventory you carry affects ROI. If inventory levels are excessive, you are at a competitive disadvantage relative to ROI unless your greater inventory investment is producing greater sales and profits than you would otherwise realize.

A good starting place in determining the reasonableness of inventory levels is the inventory turnover rate. If it is significantly lower than the industry norm, investigation is warranted. It may be that inventory control is lax or that hard-to-sell items are being carried out of reluctance to write them off. Possibly you are speculating on price increases and purchasing higher than normal amounts of raw materials. Maybe for competitive reasons you need to carry a "full line" of inventory even though it means carrying slower-moving items. All of these things contribute to inventory levels higher than those of competitors, and they all can be dragging down ROI.

A popular technique for determining an optimal amount of inventory to hold is the economic order quantity (EOQ). If you want to bring inventory levels more into line with industry norms, the EOQ formula can be helpful in identifying areas where reductions can be made.

Strengths:

- Can improve ROI

Limitations:

- May be difficult to implement
- Order costs and carrying costs assumed constant regardless of order size
- Usage assumed known
- Buffer stock not included

There are three categories of inventory investment:

1. Raw materials
2. Work-in-process
3. Finished goods

Manufacturing companies have all three types of inventory, but wholesaling and retailing companies have almost exclusively finished goods inventory.

The amount of each item held in inventory depends greatly on the expected usage, required lead time in producing or acquiring the item, and marketing considerations (such as the need to be a "full line" seller).

Inventory Management and ROI

Inventory also ties up cash. Excessive inventory will reduce ROI. Assume that companies A and B are identical in all respects except that A has more inventory for the same sales level as B does.

		A		B
Net income		$200		$200
Assets				
Cash	10		10	
Accounts receivable	300		300	
Inventory	200		100	
	510		410	
Net fixed assets	300		300	
Total assets	810		710	
ROI		25%		28%

How to Tell If Inventory Is Excessive

One way to determine whether your inventory level is excessive is to compare your inventory turnover ratio with the industry norm. If your inventory turnover is much lower than the industry average, your ROI will suffer. Let's say you have costs of goods sold of $1,000,000 and an inventory turnover of 10 times, compared to the industry average of 20 times. With these figures, your inventory investment is $10,000 when it should be $5,000. This will hurt ROI and cash.

If inventory is much higher than it should be for your level of sales, it may be that you are holding inventory that has become out of date or is simply not moving fast enough to justify its cost.

If inventory obsolescence is not a problem, check a couple of other things. For example, maybe for competitive reasons you think a full line of inventory items is essential even if some items are in very low demand. If this is the case, reevaluate the gains from this strategy relative to the ROI impact the higher investment is having.

Another possible reason for excess inventory is that you are speculating on price increases. If so, the gains from doing so should be compared to alternatives.

One manager was pleased with his ability to anticipate price increases in raw materials. He estimated his ROI on speculation to be about 20 percent per year. But actually he was having to forgo very profitable sales expansions with ROI in excess of 60 percent!

From a strictly cost standpoint, the optimal level of inventory to hold (whether completely purchased or produced in-house) involves minimizing inventory costs.

Inventory Costs

There are two basic types of inventory costs: carrying costs and ordering costs.

Carrying costs are the costs associated with storage, handling, and insurance of inventory items. The level of required ROI on the funds tied up in inventory is included as a carrying cost. On the average, the amount of inventory held will be half the amount purchased. Total carrying costs will be carrying cost per unit times half the lot size ordered.

Ordering costs are the clerical and administrative costs or set-up associated with placing an order for an item in inventory. Total ordering costs are simply the number of total orders placed in a period times the cost per order. The total number of orders placed in a period is equal to total usage divided by the quantity per order.

Relationship of Carrying Costs to Order Costs

If you expect to use 9,800 widgets over the next thirty days, you could simply buy 9,800 now and carry them in inventory until they are all used up. Or you could buy 3267 units every ten days; or you could buy smaller amounts more frequently. The more frequently you place orders for inventory, the less inventory you have to keep on hand and the less carrying costs you have. But, of course, more frequent orders result in greater ordering costs.

How to Balance Ordering Costs and Carrying Costs

Minimizing inventory cost involves balancing the carrying costs against the order costs. The economic order quantity (EOQ) formula provides a framework for balancing order and carrying costs.

In order to use the EOQ formula you need to know:

S = usage, in units expected for some period
C = carrying costs per unit expected

O = ordering costs
Q = optimal size of order to place

$$Q = \sqrt{\frac{2SO}{C}}$$

You expect to use 9,800 widgets over the next thirty days. Order costs are $100 per order. Carrying costs for thirty days are $1 per widget.

$$Q = \sqrt{\frac{(2) \times (9,800) \times (100)}{1}} = 1400$$

Interpretation of EOQ Formula

The EOQ formula in the above example says that you should order 1,400 widgets at a time. This means placing seven orders during the thirty days, or about one every four days.

Total carrying costs = (1400/2) 1 = $700
Total ordering costs = (7.0) 100 = $700

Notice that this is the same as minimizing total costs, as shown in Table 22.1. Figure 22.1 graphically illustrates the relationship of inventory costs to quantity ordered.

Figure 22.1   Relationship of Inventory to Quantity Ordered

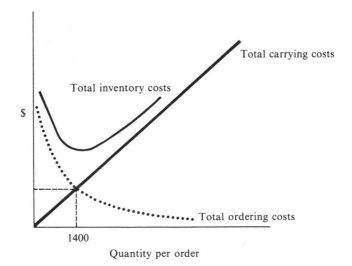

TABLE 22.1. Relationship of Inventory Costs to Quantity Ordered

Lot Size per Order	No. Orders	Average Inventory	Total Order Costs	Total Carrying Costs	Total Inventory Costs
900	10.9	450	$1088.89	450	$1538.89
1000	9.8	500	980.00	500	1480.00
1100	8.91	550	890.91	550	1440.91
1200	8.17	600	816.67	600	1416.67
1300	7.54	650	753.85	650	1403.85
1400	7.00	700	700.00	700	1400.00
1500	6.53	750	653.33	750	1403.33
1600	6.13	800	612.50	800	1412.50

Things to Watch Out For

The EOQ formula is important primarily in identifying the cost factors involved in inventory investment. But the simple formula involves a number of important assumptions that should be recognized:

- Order costs and carrying costs assumed constant regardless of order size
- Usage assumed known
- Buffer stock not included

## PART FIVE

Capital Budgeting

Among its investment decisions, the capital budgeting decisions represent the most strategic to the company for several reasons:

- They determine your ROI potential.
- They affect the business character of the company.
- They are multiyear investments.
- They are often hard and costly to reverse.
- They are "lumpy," often involving relatively large amounts of corporate funds.
- They are exposed to considerable risks, which cannot be easily evaluated.

Without undertaking such investment decisions and risks, many firms could not continue in their lines of business.

Topics Covered in This Part

This part discusses the process of identifying and selecting multiyear investments. The following chapters are included:

Types of Capital Budgeting Proposals

Most capital budgeting proposals can be placed in one of the following categories:

    • *Strategic* investments, which are considered necessary to maintain the existing lines of business and/or preserve market share. This includes *replacement and maintenance* investments, which are sometimes called "defensive" investments. Such investments often escape financial scrutiny, since they are considered essential or have benefits that can not be accurately quantified.

    • *Cost reduction* investments.

    • *Growth and expansion* investments, which are proposed investments in new markets and/or products or involve increased commitments to existing lines of business. Investments in this group are considered to carry the most risk.

Capital Budgeting Process

The actual capital budgeting process varies substantially from one firm to another. In most large firms many capital budgeting decisions are made at the plant and division levels, with only the largest and riskiest investments decided by the board of directors. In large companies it is not unusual, for example, for investment proposals up to $100,000 to be made at the division manager level.

    As major investment proposals begin to climb the capital budgeting ladder, their formation and evaluation become increasingly detailed. Corporations will normally have fairly detailed manuals for the preparation and evaluation of investment proposals.

Capital Budgeting Techniques

There are several capital budgeting techniques in use. Each technique emphasizes a different aspect of the investment decision. For this reason, the various techniques should be considered complementary rather than competing. It is generally agreed that from an academic standpoint the *discounted cash flow* techniques are the most reliable measures of an investment's economic value. However other methods, especially the *average* (or accountant's) *rate of return* and the *payback period* are commonly used, even though they might not reveal a project's true economic value.

Data Requirements

Data requirements depend on the technique to be adopted. Generally, there must be information on the expected total amount of the investment, financing mix and costs, the expected duration of the investment, expected profits and the timing of profits over the life of the investment, and the standard to be used in accepting or rejecting the proposal.

In addition to the quantitative data needed, there should also be information on the many important but qualitative factors, such as the "fit" of the investment with the company's other investments, the compatibility of the investment with corporate objectives and managerial abilities. There must also be concern for the competitive environment and the evolving business environment.

Investment Outlays

The amount of investment outlay can usually be estimated with a high degree of accuracy. The investment base should include not only outlays for plant and equipment required to produce output but also any working capital needed, such as cash for operations, accounts receivable to support sales, and the level of inventories needed to support production and sales.

Over the life of the investment, the plant and equipment will decrease through depreciation. The amount of working capital will not depreciate, but it will vary with the rise and fall of sales and production activities.

A decrease in the investment base represents a cash inflow as the investment is recovered. An increase in investment represents an additional commitment of cash and represents a cash outflow.

To avoid unnecessarily complicating this presentation, we will assume that working capital investments are made at the beginning of the investment life and do not change. They are recovered in full at the end of the investment. We will also assume that the depreciable assets (such as plant and equipment) are depreciated over the investment's life to a zero value.

Estimating Investment Returns

The returns for a proposed investment can be estimated with pro forma statements covering each period of the investment's life. However, these investment pro formas differ from the usual pro forma and audited statements in some important ways. These are taken up below.

Investment Returns: Cash Flow
Versus Net Income

The "returns" from an investment include not only the profits earned through the investment but also the recovery of the investment base itself. As cash is recovered from an investment it is available for reinvestment elsewhere.

Profits and depreciation should be added together to measure the investment's cash flow. Profits represent the return *on* investment; depreciation represents the recovery (return) *of* investment.

It would be incorrect to call depreciation a source of cash, but treat it as if it were. Here's why:

Consider a company that makes all sales on cash basis and pays all expenses (except depreciation, which, recall, is a noncash accounting charge-off) in cash:

Income Statement		*Actual Cash Balance*		
(1) Sales	$1,000	(1)	+	$1,000
(2) CGS	600	(2)	−	600
Gross profit	400			
(3) Oper. expenses	200	(3)	−	200
Depreciation exp.	**100**			
Profit before taxes	100			
(4) Taxes (50%)	50	(4)	−	50
Net income	**$50**	**Cash balance**		**$150**

Net income is $50 but the actual cash balance is $150. The difference is the $100 of depreciation, which reduced net income but not the cash account.

Therefore, from this investment, the full returns this year are $150, of which $50 (net income) represents return *on* investment and $100 (depreciation) represents return *of* investment.

Although it is a recovery of investment, depreciation increases returns because it provides a shield against taxes. In other words, it reduces the amount of taxes you have to pay but does not reduce the amount of cash you have.

Assume that depreciation is *not* deductible for tax purposes. With the same sales and expenses of the previous example, notice that taxes increase from $50 to $100. So total cash generated from the investment becomes only $100 instead of $150.

Income Statement		*Actual Cash Balance*	
(1) Sales	$1,000	(1) + $1,000	
(2) CGS	600	(2) − 600	
Gross profit	400		
(3) Oper Expenses	200	(3) − 200	
Deprec. (not tx deduct)			
Profits before taxes	100		
(4) Taxes	100	(4) − 100	
Net income	**$100**	**Actual cash balance $100**	

When depreciation is not tax deductible, net income is higher: $100 instead of $50, but this is very misleading. Total returns are now only $100 instead of $150 as in the earlier example.

Summary of Depreciation Examples

	Depreciation Tax Deductible	*Depreciation Non–Tax Deductible*
Net income	$50	$100
Cash flow	$150	$100
Recovery *of* investment	− 100	− 100
Return *on* investment	$50	0

As you can clearly see, without the tax shield of depreciation, in this example (though not always), there is ZERO return on investment even though profits are "higher."

Incremental Cash Flow

In a replacement proposal, net income and depreciation cash flows will be generated by the proposed investment. However, existing earnings potential and depreciation will be lost if the replacement proposal is accepted. In such proposals, therefore, only the net change in cash flows is considered. Most simply this is calculated as:

Incremental cash flow = New cash flow − Old cash flow

Of course, in a replacement decision there will be salvage or trade-in value from the existing investment base. Only the net increase in investment should be considered.

Incremental investment = New investment − Sale value of
old investment

Unlevering the Investment

If debt is to be used as part of the financing of the proposed investment, interest expenses will be generated, and these would normally be incorporated in pro forma income statements. However, in the investment proposal it is important to keep interest expenses *off* the statement for a couple of reasons:

1. Including interest expenses will reduce the comparability of different proposals. Interest expense will reduce the projected cash flow. But the amount of debt financing to be used may vary randomly from investment to investment, depending on whether and how much debt happens to be available rather than the investment value itself.

2. As will become clearer, deducting interest expense involves "double-counting" investment costs. The returns projected for the investment will be compared with the costs of financing the project. If the cost of financing (i.e., interest expense) is deducted from the return, this will double-count the financing cost.

For these reasons, the cash flows projected for investments should not show interest expense. In other words, the investment aspect should be kept separate from the financing aspect.

## 23

The Capital Budgeting Objective

EXECUTIVE SUMMARY

The primary objective of capital budgeting is to allocate scarce corporate funds among competing investment proposals in a manner that increases the value of the company.

Finance can contribute importantly to the capital budgeting objective by comparing the returns from investments with their costs. Among the four methods most frequently used, only the present value and internal rate of return methods are reliable for determining the acceptability of investments and in ranking them on the basis of economic value.

In terms of economic value, an investment is acceptable only if its compound average return on investment equals or exceeds the compound average cost of investment funds.

The primary objective of capital budgeting is to determine which investment opportunities are worth undertaking and which are not. In the event all acceptable investments cannot be undertaken, capital budgeting also involves ranking investments in order of preferability.

Identification of Acceptable Investments

There are four principal methods used to identify acceptable investments:

- The average rate of return method (ARR)
- The payback method (PB)
- The present value method (PV)
- The internal rate of return method (IRR)

This book has continuously stressed the importance of ROI as the primary financial objective of the business. Given that objective, an investment is acceptable if it will provide an overall ROI that meets or exceeds some minimal level of ROI performance over its life.

Among the methods listed, only the present value and internal rate of return methods are reliable for determining the acceptability of investments and in ranking them in order of desirability. The average rate of return method is popular because, in spite of its weaknesses, it is easy to use and often provides a close approximation to the real profitability of the investment. The payback method is also popular because it is easy to use. Unlike the other methods, payback is not directly concerned with the ROI of the investment. Payback is a "safety first" method that tries to identify those investments with the fastest investment recovery.

The Minimum Acceptable ROI

The cost of funds employed in making investments determines the minimum acceptable ROI. If funds cost you 15 percent and you invest in projects whose returns are 10 percent, you will lose 5 percent on the investment, on the average, every year of the investment's life. The minimum acceptable ROI from an investment is known as the cost of capital of the investment.

A common misconception is that the cost of capital is the same thing as the cost of debt funds (i.e., the interest cost of debt). However, the proper calculation of the cost of capital should take into account all the sources of financing used by the firm, including preferred stock and owners' equity. When the costs of all these financing sources are considered, the cost of capital is a weighted average of the individual costs.

The cost of capital is the subject of Part VI of the book, but you should keep in mind that the cost of capital is the minimum acceptable ROI performance from an investment. In particular, any deviation from the minimum level of return is absorbed by the owners of the company: If the investment's ROI is greater than the minimum, share-holders (owners) get higher returns than expected and the value of the company increases. If the investment's ROI is less than the minimum, shareholders get lower returns than they expected and the value of the company decreases.

Investment Selection

Assume that the cost of capital for all investments is 10 percent. You are considering the following six investment proposals:

			Decision	
Investment	$Outlays	ROI	Accept	Reject
# 1	$1,000	20%	X	
# 2	$2,000	18%	X	
# 3	$3,000	16%	X	
# 4	$4,000	8%		X
# 5	$5,000	5%		X
# 6	$6,000	12%	X	

Among available investments, investments # 1, # 2, # 3, and # 6 are acceptable, and # 4 and # 5 are unacceptable. Among the acceptable investments, a ranking on the basis of ROI would produce the following order:

Rank	Investment	$Outlays	ROI
1	# 1	$1,000	20%
2	# 2	$2,000	18%
3	# 3	$3,000	16%
4	# 6	$6,000	12%
	Total	$12,000	

Capital Rationing

Capital rationing occurs whenever you have more acceptable investments than you can undertake. For example, the four investments identified as acceptable will require a total investment budget of $12,000. What if you only have $6,000 available for investment? Should you take on investments # 1, # 2, and # 3, or investment # 6 only? In either case, the total investment required will be $6,000, just equal to what you have to spend.

In this example, the correct choice is clearly undertaking investments # 1, # 2, and # 3 since every one of the investments in the collection has a higher ROI than investment # 6.

Mutually Exclusive Investments

Even if you had the funds to undertake all acceptable investments ($12,000), you may not be able to if any of them are mutually exclusive. This occurs whenever the acceptance of one investment requires rejection of another investment. For example, what if investments # 1 and # 2 are two alternative production processes? If you choose process # 1, you can't also use process # 2. In other words, mutually exclusive choices are like selecting what tie to wear: If you choose one you imply rejection of all the others.

Average ROI

Calculating the ROI from a one-year investment is relatively easy, you simply take a ratio of the "profit" over the "investment," just as we've done throughout this book.

A complication arises when you consider investments for more than a year. The ROI from one year may be unacceptable, but the following year the ROI may be extremely high. In order to determine whether, overall, the investment will meet your minimal ROI target, you need to get an average of the investment's ROI over its entire life.

For example, recall that investment # 1 had the highest ROI (20%) over its life. The 20 percent represents the average annual ROI that you will realize from the investment over its entire life. Assume that investment # 1 has the following ROIs over a three-year life:

Investment # 1

Year	1	2	3
ROI	5%	20%	37%

What is the average ROI from investment # 1? There are basically two different ways to calculate it: simple average or compound average. The 20 percent given earlier was calculated on a compound average basis. The compound average basis is a little more complicated than the simple ROI average basis, but I think you will readily see that the compound average basis is what you are more accustomed to. The compound return basis, of course, is the method used and advertised for bank savings accounts and accounts at thrift institutions.

Simple Versus Compound Average ROI: An Illustration

The best way to grasp the difference between simple and compound average ROI is to consider two alternative investments. Assume that investments A and B both require investment outlays of $200 and this is the average investment outstanding. Assume that they both have the pattern of profits shown below:

Year	1	2	3	4	5	Total	Average Profit
A	0	$10	$20	$30	$190	$250	$50
B	$140	$10	$20	$30	0	$200	$40

Assuming average investments of $200 for each alternative, we get the following overall average ROI:

	Average Profit	Average Investment	Simple Average ROI
A	$50	$200	25%
B	$40	$200	20%

Let's assume that you and I are rival managers. We are both considering the same investments. You take investment A because it has the greater average ROI and greater total profits ($250 compared to $200 for B). I take investment B because, even though I get less return than you do, I get it faster. And because of that simple fact I will be able to outperform you in every year!

How I Will Outperform You

Here's the "trick." Because I get money back sooner, I can turn around and reinvest it somewhere else while you're still waiting for yours to come in. In the first year I get $140 in profits while you get zero. Let's say I can invest at 15 percent after taxes. I will take that $140 from year one and invest it. In year two I get $10 from the original investment (B) *plus* $21 more after taxes from the reinvestment of my $140. So in year two I will produce total profits of $31 compared to your $10. At the end of year two I will have $171 in cash compared to your $10. My $171 now generates an additional $25.65 in year three, and so on, while the $10 you received in year two contributes (at 15 percent) $1.50. By the end of the fifth year, I end up with $321 compared to your $266.

In other words, by *compounding* my investment return I actually ended up with a more profitable investment. Thus, compound average ROI is a better way to select investments. There are two compound ROI methods: net present value and internal rate of return. The average (or accountants') rate of return method is *not* a compound ROI method and is thus an unreliable way to select investments. The fourth method discussed in this chapter, the payback method, is not an explicit ROI method at all.

## 24

Average (Accountant's) Rate of Return (ARR)

EXECUTIVE SUMMARY

The average (accountant's) rate of return (ARR) method is one of the most popular methods of capital budgeting used. Its main virtues are that it employs the accounting definition of ROI used in evaluating the firm's overall performance and it is easy to calculate. The biggest problem with the ARR technique is that it is a *simple average* rather than a *compound* ROI method. This can seriously distort the real profitability of a long-lived investment or one whose returns are not uniform over the life of the investment. Adding to this weakness is that the ARR method ignores the pattern of cash flows generated by the recovery of the investment (i.e. depreciation).

Strengths:

- Simple to calculate
- A single measure

- Related to performance measure
- Readily understood
- Related to cost of funds
- Adjusted for scale of investment
- Allows ranking of alternatives

Limitations:

- As an average, hides data
- Investment basis not defined
- Ignores timing of full returns

Because of its importance in evaluating historical performance, the accounting version of ROI is commonly employed as a technique for selecting investments. One version of this method is known as the average rate of return (ARR).

ARR is calculated as the *ratio of average profits after taxes to average investment.* When used in capital budgeting decisions, ARR is calculated for each investment proposal, producing a summary percentage rate of return. All investment proposals are then ranked, and the most profitable ones are accepted.

You are considering the following investments. Because of a limited capital budget you will only be able to select one of the two:

	Investment	
	Cost Reduction (# 1)	*New Product (# 2)*
Average investment	$1,000	$1,000
Average profits after taxes (per year)	100	150
ARR	**10%**	**15%**

Investment #2 has a superior ARR and therefore seems preferable. The implication of the calculation is that if you undertake investment #2, year-to-year ROI, on the average will be 15 percent.

Strengths of the Simple ROI Method

- *Simple to calculate.* Of considerable importance, ARR is easily calculated. Requiring little information beyond typical accounting data, approximations can be developed quickly. As a ratio of two numbers, profits and investments, both of which tie back into financial statements, there is no hidden "massaging" of the numbers or adjustments involving (possibly arguable) judgments.

• *A single measure.* This technique produces a single, summary measure of profitability that can be compared with all other competing proposals but, equally important, also can be compared with historical performance or otherwise related to the corporate-wide ROI "target."

• *Related to performance measure.* Another substantial attraction of this technique is that it selects investments in a manner consistent with the evaluation of later performance. As we have already seen, year-to-year ROI performance is often used as a measure of operating performance for project managers and for the company overall. Selecting investments on this basis provides a consistent measure.

• *Readily understood and communicated throughout the company.* Since corporate management is geared to thinking of profitability in percentage return terms, use of ROI as a method of project selection is intuitively more acceptable to operating management and further reinforces the role of ROI in evaluation of operating performance.

• *Can be related to cost of funds.* A percentage ROI hurdle (minimum acceptable rate) can be justified easily with comparison to the average percentage cost of funds raised by the company. As noted earlier, also, a minimum acceptable standard based on previous performance (such as average realized performance for the last two years) is also intuitively acceptable.

• *Adjusted for the scale of investment.* Percentage return allows comparison of projects with different investment requirements and differing lives. The ARR calculation is a ratio and as such is automatically adjusted for the scale of investment. An investment with an ARR of 20 percent provides twice as much return on the investment dollar as one with an ARR of 10 percent, regardless of the number of dollars invested.

• *Allows ranking of alternatives.* When there are more projects than cash available, the ARR method allows the most profitable ones to be identified. In choosing between mutually exclusive investments the ROI method allows comparison on the basis of expected returns as they will be reported in financial statements. As noted before, when a cutoff rate or hurdle rate is used, the ranking procedure allows quick selection of the most attractive investments.

Limitations of the ARR Method

Unfortunately, there are several serious shortcomings in the ARR method. The most severe is that it is not a reliable measure of investment *value*. This is primarily because it ignores crucial determinants of an investment's value.

    • *As an average it hides data.* There may be very great volatility in actual reported results on a year-to-year basis. This volatility is disguised in the averaging process. Let's take a dramatic example. Let's say the investment lasts five years and the year-to-year results are:

			Year				
	1	2	3	4	5	Total	Average
Net income							
Investment # 1	$100	$100	$100	$100	$100	$500	$100
Investment # 2	− $100	− $200	− $300	$100	$1250	$750	$150

This is a considerably different picture. Will shareholders be willing to wait out the miserable performance during the first four years of investment # 2 in hopes of getting the fifth year bonanza (which they are unlikely even to forsee)? As important, will you survive the first three years of investment # 2? If compensation is related to ROI, will you even be willing to try? And what about the impacts on reported earnings per share? Let's say you check into this (for simplicity, ignore all other investments the company has; assume that there are 100 shares of stock outstanding).

			Year		
	1	2	3	4	5
Earnings per share					
Investment # 1	$1.00	$1.00	$1.00	$1.00	$1.00
Investment # 2	d	d	d	$1.00	$12.50
(d-deficit)					

In short, the averaging process conceals a lot of potentially crucial information.

    • *Ignores the timing of full returns.* The ARR method considers only profits and ignores the other part of cash flow: recovery of investment through depreciation charges against net income. Since the timing of cash flows is important to investment value, this is a serious shortcoming.

## 25

Payback (PB) Method

EXECUTIVE SUMMARY

The payback method is very popular for two principal reasons:

- It is easy to calculate
- It emphasizes concern for investment safety

The basic question addressed by the payback method is: How long before I get my money back? Nothing is said about profits explicitly, although you would normally expect investments that have very short paybacks to be unusually profitable. However, the payback method is just not very reliable for purposes of identifying the most profitable investments. It is best used in conjunction with other discounted cash flow methods.

Strengths:

- Easily understood
- Easy to calculate

- Favors short investments
- Considers cash flows
- Crude estimate of profitability
- Does not depend on scale of investment
- A single measure
- Allows ranking of alternatives

Limitations:

- Hides a lot of data
- Does not explicitly measure profits
- Unreliable guide to proper decisions

A measure that does employ cash flow instead of net income in measuring the returns to investors is the payback method. The payback method does not directly measure profitability; it is simply a measure of the length of time until the original investment is recovered.

If an investment's payback period is 3.5 years, the initial investment will be recovered in three and a half years. If the payback period exceeds the applicable standard, the investment is rejected; otherwise, it is accepted.

Riskier investments usually will be required to have shorter paybacks than safer investments. For a given level of risk, the shorter the payback, the more attractive the investment is. In certain cases the payback method is a crude but indirect measure of "profitability" in the following sense: If payback is two years (i.e., it will take two years to recover the original investment), the profitability of the investment must be very high (close to 50 percent per year).

But notice that the payback method gives no clues as to how "profitable" the investment will be in year three and thereafter.

Payback is also a crude measure of risk, since the faster the payback (the shorter the payback period), the less exposure there is to future uncertainties. For this reason, you can see why it is a popular method in practice—it focuses on cash and the immediacy of investment recovery. Even though there is some indirect suggestion of "risk" based on the length of the payback period, there is no direct recognition of the fact that riskiness may vary substantially among otherwise comparable payback periods. Assume that an investment costs $100 and has the following cash flows:

Year	1	2	3	4	5
Cash flow	28	25	23	40	25

It will take between three and four years to recover the original investment. At the end of the third year only $76 of the original $100 has been recovered. At the end of the fourth year, $116 will have been recovered. Entering the fourth year only $24 has to be recovered. Since this represents about 60 percent (i.e. $25/40) of the cash flow in the fourth year, the payback period on this investment is about 3.6 years.

The payback method has a strong advantage over the ARR method in identifying those investments which will provide cash flows earliest. However, a major disadvantage of the payback method is that it really ignores overall profitability from the investment. For example, an investment with very large cash inflows in year 5 might be rejected simply because its payback period exceeds 4 years.

## 26

Present Value (PV) Method

EXECUTIVE SUMMARY

The present value method answers a very simple but strategic investment question: "How much should I pay for this investment if I want to be sure of making___percent return on investment?"

If you consider any particular investment with the present value method you will discover that the maximum amount you should pay for the investment depends on the rate of return you are looking for. In other words, for a given investment, the higher your required return on investment, the less you should pay for the investment, and vice versa.

The present value of an investment is the *maximum* you can afford to pay for the investment and still earn your required rate of return.

This is not so surprising when you realize that this is the

same thing as saying, "The less you pay for an investment, the greater your profit is going to be."

Strengths:

- The most reliable valuation method
- Explicitly incorporates your desired ROI
- A compound ROI (discounted cash flow) method
- Can be easily calculated once data are assembled
- Directly relates cost of capital to investment value

Limitations:

- Deceptive air of precision
- Much greater data requirements about investment
- Requires estimate of costs of capital
- Does not directly relate to year-to-year performance as reported
- Does not indicate "true" ROI—only whether it is more or less than prespecified amount
- Not readily understood or communicated

The present value (PV) method of capital budgeting is designed to calculate the value of an investment given the expected cash flows the investment will produce over its life and your desire to earn a predetermined compound ROI over the life of the investment.

The PV method uses a scientific technique known as *discounting*. This technique produces a set of *discount factors,* which are applied to the cash flows expected from the investment in order to determine their value, given that you require a specified ROI. A table of discount factors, such as the one in the back of this book, can be easily used in applying the PV method. In addition, even inexpensive hand-held calculators are programmed by the manufacturer to calculate present values quickly.

An excerpt from a discount factor table is shown in Table 26.1. The first column contains the number of periods before you receive the cash flow. The remaining columns indicate a range of expected ROI rates. The numbers inside the table are the discount factors, which you apply to the cash flows from the investment.

TABLE 26.1. Discount Factor Table, ROI/Year

Period	1%	2%	4%	6%	8%	10%	12%	14%	15%	16%	18%	20%
1	0.990	0.980	0.962	0.943	0.926	0.909	0.893	0.877	0.870	0.862	0.847	0.833
2	0.980	0.961	0.925	0.890	0.857	0.826	0.797	0.769	0.756	0.743	0.718	0.694
3	0.971	0.942	0.889	0.840	0.794	0.751	0.712	0.675	0.658	0.641	0.609	0.579
4	0.961	0.924	0.855	0.792	0.735	0.683	0.636	0.592	0.572	0.552	0.516	0.482
5	0.951	0.906	0.822	0.747	0.681	0.621	0.567	0.519	0.497	0.476	0.437	0.402
6	0.942	0.888	0.790	0.705	0.630	0.564	0.507	0.456	0.432	0.410	0.370	0.335
7	0.933	0.871	0.760	0.665	0.583	0.513	0.452	0.400	0.376	0.354	0.314	0.279
8	0.923	0.853	0.731	0.627	0.540	0.467	0.404	0.351	0.327	0.305	0.266	0.233
9	0.914	0.837	0.703	0.592	0.500	0.424	0.361	0.308	0.284	0.263	0.225	0.194
10	0.905	0.820	0.676	0.558	0.463	0.386	0.322	0.270	0.247	0.227	0.191	0.162

Assume that you are considering an investment that will produce the following cash flows over its three-year life:

Year	1	2	3
Cash flow	$100	$200	$300

Assume that you want a 10 percent compound ROI from the investment. How much is the investment worth? To calculate this, obtain the discount factor from the table for each year, multiply the discount factor times the cash flow, and add up all the discounted cash flows. The total represents the value of the investment:

Year	1	2	3	
Cash flow	$100	$200	$300	
Discount factor @ 10%	.909	.826	.751	
Discounted cash flow	$90.90	$165.20	$225.30	
Total discounted cash flow (present value)				$481.40

How to Interpret the Discounted Cash Flow

The discounted cash flow represents the value of the investment. If you were to pay $481.40 right now for the investment with the cash flows described, you would realize a compound return on investment of 10 percent per year over the investment's life.

The $481.40 value of the investment is called its *present value*. If the investment's cost exceeds its present value, you should not undertake it. If the investment's cost is less than its present value, you should undertake it, since you will pay less for the investment than it is worth to you. If the investment's cost is just equal to its present value, you should still undertake it, because even though you are paying for the investment what it is worth to you, you are getting the compound ROI you desire.

Net Present Value

Net present value is determined by subtracting the cost of an investment from its present value.

Net present value = Total present value − Investment cost

Assume that the investment cost is $400 and that the total present value of cash inflows, at a 10 percent ROI, is $481.40. The net present value is then $81.40.

$$\begin{aligned} \text{Net present value} &= \text{Total present value} - \text{Investment cost} \\ &= \$481.40 - 400 \\ &= \$81.40 \end{aligned}$$

Present Value Is Negatively Related to Time

A look at the discount factor table reveals something else of great importance. The discount factors decrease the farther into the future cash flows are received. In other words, the present value of an investment's cash flows will decrease the longer you have to wait for them. Assume that instead of receiving cash flows in years one, two, and three you will not receive any cash flows until years four, five, and six. Notice what happens to the discount factors (they get smaller), the discounted cash flows (they get smaller), and the total present value (it gets smaller):

Year	1	2	3	4	5	6	
Cash flows	0	0	0	$100	$200	$300	
Discount factor @ 10%	.909	.826	.751	.683	.621	.564	
Discounted cash flow	0	0	0	$68.30	$124.20	$169.20	
Total discounted cash flow (present value)							$361.70

The present value of the three cash flows has dropped from $481.40 to only $361.70, since the cash flows have been delayed until years four, five, and six.

The moral is, the longer it takes to get the cash, the less the investment's worth to you.

Present Value Is Negatively Related to ROI

For a given investment's cash flows, the higher the ROI you want from the investment, the less its present value. To see this, think back to the original investment with its cash flows in years one, two, and three. In the earlier example I used a 10 percent required ROI, and the total present value was $481.40. However, if I required an ROI, of 20 percent per year from the investment, its present value would only be $395.80.

Notice that at the higher ROI the discount factors decrease, the discounted cash flows decrease, and the present value decreases:

Year	1	2	3	
Cash flows	$100	$200	$300	
Discount factor @ 20%	.833	.694	.579	
Discounted cash flow	$83.30	$138.80	$173.70	
Total present value				$395.80

The moral is, the greater your required return, the less you should pay for a given investment.

## 27

Profitability Index

EXECUTIVE SUMMARY

Net present value comparisons among equally acceptable projects are biased by the scale of investment: we expect large projects to have large cash flows and small projects to have small cash flows.

The profitability index is a way of adjusting cash flows by the scale of investment required. The result can be interpreted as the present value per dollar of investment required. More profitable investments have higher profitablity index values than less profitable investments.

The profitability index is used in situations of capital rationing or when otherwise acceptable investments turn out to be mutually exclusive.

Generally, the net present value (NPV) method will be the most reliable financial guide to investment decisions if all investments with positive net present values can be undertaken. However, when a company must ration capital because it has more acceptable investments than money available, or when a company is considering mutually exclusive investments, the simple calculation of NPV may not be enough.

Consider the following set of possible investments. Assume that they are all mutually exclusive: To adopt one means that none of the others can be adopted.

Project	Investment	NPV
A	$100	$20
B	$500	$75
C	$1000	$100

Investment C has the most NPV, but is it the most profitable? Investment C has five times the NPV of A but requires ten times as much investment. Net present value alone does not take the size of investments into account directly and therefore must be modified when used for comparisons such as these. The *profitability index* is a method for modifying the present value calculations.

The profitability index is a ratio of the present value of cash inflows to the level of investment. In this way the profitability index tells us how much present value is generated for each dollar of investment. The higher the profitability index, the more profitable the investment is.

Project	Investment	Present Value	Profitability Index
A	$100	$120	1.20
B	$500	$575	1.15
C	$1000	$1100	1.10

When the present value of the investment is equal to the cost of the investment, net present value is zero and the profitability index is 1.0. When net present value is negative, the profitability index is less than

1.0. When net present value is positive, the profitability index is greater than 1.0.

The profitability index provides a means of ranking investments on the basis of relative profitability but does not indicate exactly how profitable the investment really is in ROI terms. The focus on exact profitability is the objective of internal rate of return (IRR) analysis.

## 28

Internal Rate of Return (IRR)

EXECUTIVE SUMMARY

The internal rate of return method is another type of discounted cash flow technique. It employs the same information as the net present value method but answers a different question about the investment: "If I undertake the investment, what overall return on investment will I receive?"

The IRR method, like the PV method, separates cash flows into their two components:

- Return *on* investment
- Recovery *of* investment

While the PV method "locks in" some target compound ROI and then calculates the value of an investment recovered, the IRR method takes a different approach. The IRR method assumes a value for an investment and then calculates how much "profit" is left over in the cash flows each year.

Strengths:

- Very reliable valuation method
- Direct measure of an investment's "true" ROI
- Related to performance measure
- Can be directly compared to cost of funds
- A compound ROI (discounted cash flow) method
- Adjusted for scale of investment
- Allows ranking of alternatives
- Not hard to calculate once data are assembled

Limitations:

- Deceptive air of precision
- Much greater requirements for investment data
- Requires estimate of costs of capital
- As an average over entire investment life, does not directly relate to reported year-to-year performance

---

The present value method attempts to determine the value of an investment given its cash flows and given some prespecified ROI. The internal rate of return method attempts to determine the actual ROI from an investment given its cash flows and a predetermined value. The "predetermined value" is the cost of the investment.

The IRR from an investment is the ROI that results in a present value equal to the cost of the investment.

In other words, the present value and internal rate of return methods are alternative methods for evaluating the same investment. They simply try to answer different questions.

If I were to tell you that investment X has a positive net present value given a return of 10 percent, you could conclude that the actual ROI of the investment was more than 10 percent, but you would not know whether the real ROI was 12 percent, 15 percent, 20 percent, or what.

For a number of reasons, we are often more interested in knowing exactly what ROI we will realize from an investment rather than simply whether it will be more or less than some assumed rate.

The essential task in IRR analysis is to find the ROI whose discount factors result in a total present value equal to the cost of the investment (i.e., produce a net present value equal to zero). The ROI that produces this zero NPV is the internal rate of return on the investment.

By *trial and error* you have to use different ROI rates to find that rate which produces a net present value of zero.

Selection by IRR

If the investment's IRR exceeds its required rate of return, the investment should be accepted. If the investment's IRR is less than the required rate of return, the investment should be rejected. If the IRR is just equal to the required rate of return, the investment should be accepted, because it will provide just the level of ROI required.

An important feature of the IRR method is that it permits a ranking of alternative investments on the basis of maximum ROI. When there are insufficient funds to undertake all investments or when you must choose between mutually exclusive investments, the ROI ranking will help in the selection decision.

Calculation of IRR

Assume the same investment that we examined in the PV discussion. Assume the investment costs $395.80. What is its IRR? Remember that "the IRR from an investment is the ROI that results in a present value equal to the cost of the investment." By trial and error let us try ROIs of 10, 15, and 20 percent to see which is closest to a net present value of zero. As you can see from Table 28.1, the investment has an IRR of 20 percent. You know this because an ROI of 20 percent will produce a net present value of zero.

How to Interpret IRR

The IRR tells you what ROI you will actually earn from an investment given its costs and cash flows. If you undertake the investment, given its cost of $395.80, you will earn a compound ROI of 20 percent per year.

If the investment in Table 28.1 had actually cost $435.60 instead of $395.80, notice that its IRR would have been 15 percent rather than 20 percent; if the investment had cost $481.40, the IRR would have only been 10 percent.

TABLE 28.1 Calculation of IRR

Year	Cash Flow	ROI 10% Discount Factor	ROI 10% Present Value	ROI 15% Discount Factor	ROI 15% Present Value	ROI 20% Discount Factor	ROI 20% Present Value
1	100	.904	90.90	.870	87.00	.833	83.30
2	200	.826	165.20	.756	151.20	.694	138.80
3	300	.751	225.30	.658	197.40	.579	173.70
Total present value			$481.40		$435.60		$395.80
Minus investment cost			− 395.80		− 395.80		− 395.80
= Net present value			$ 85.60		$ 39.80		$0
IRR		Greater than 10%		Greater than 15%		Exactly 20%	

206

## 29

Other Capital Budgeting Techniques

EXECUTIVE SUMMARY

The capital budgeting methods examined so far do not handle risk in systematic ways. Two techniques which focus directly on the dispersion of investment outcomes are discussed in this chapter: decision tree analysis and simulation analysis. These techniques have important limitations of their own, however, principally the complexity required in estimating the range and probabilities of different investment outcomes. They are most useful for the analysis of investments of strategic importance to the company.

In addition to the techniques examined so far, there are two other important methods: (1) decision tree analysis and (2) risk (simulation) analysis.

Decision Trees

A weakness in ARR, payback, IRR, and NPV analyses is that they represent overall investment composites—a single summary measure of the investment rather than the range of possible outcomes. But the range of possible outcomes can be of crucial importance if one of those outcomes is disastrous to the company. In other words, extreme outcomes are "hidden" in the techniques we have discussed so far. The decision tree approach is directed toward specifying possible outcomes and the range of those outcomes contained in investment proposals.

Strengths

The principal virtue of decision tree analysis is that it permits certain outcomes to be specified and also permits specific estimates of the probability of their occurrence.

Limitations

A major weakness of the decision tree method is that it is impossible to use when many possible outcomes are considered, when many time periods are involved, or when many of the outcomes are interdependent—in other words, in most investment decisions. Because it is unwieldy, decision tree analysis is reserved for major untried investments where a careful enumeration of risks is of particular importance. For such decisions, even gross approximations of outcomes and probabilities may provide much information.

Risk Analysis

Risk analysis is a formalization and a computerization of decision tree analysis. By employing simulation techniques in projecting investment outcomes, risk analysis permits the incorporation of infinitely more possible outcomes than would decision tree analysis alone. In some cases, interrelationships among outcomes can be incorporated in risk analysis, thus compensating for another important weakness in decision tree analysis. However, such interdependences are hard to handle, and progress in this area is very limited.

## 30

A Capital Budgeting Example

EXECUTIVE SUMMARY

This chapter provides a comprehensive illustration of a capital budgeting evaluation employing the four most popular investment techniques.

The following investment proposal is presented to you:

- Type of investment: machine
- Investment outlay required: $250,000
- Investment life: five years
- Depreciation method: straight-line
- Required rate of return: 20 percent per year, compounded

Step 1. Estimate profits each year. Assume that you have developed pro forma income statements for each of the five years (see Table 30.1) and that the pro formas indicate the following net income for each of the five years.

Year	1	2	3	4	5	Total
Net income ($000)	− 10	50	160	100	25	325

Step 2. Estimate cash flow per year. Depreciation on a straight-line basis will be $\frac{\$250,000}{5} = \$50,000$ per year. Cash flow is equal to net income plus depreciation each year. Adding these together, we obtain the figures on the "Cash flow" line at the bottom of Table 30.1.

TABLE 30.1.   Pro Forma Statements: Capital Budgeting Proposal ($000)

	Year				
	1	2	3	4	5
Sales	120	600	1480	1000	400
Cost of goods sold (60%)	72	360	888	600	240
Gross profit (40%)	48	240	592	400	160
Other Expenses					
Selling	6	30	74	50	20
General & administrative	12	60	148	100	40
Depreciation	50	50	50	50	50
EBIT					
Interest	(omit to avoid double-counting)				
EBT	(20)	100	320	200	50
Taxes (50%)	(10)	50	160	100	25
Net income	(10)	50	160	100	25
Net income	(10)	50	160	100	25
Plus depreciation	50	50	50	50	50
Cash flow	40	100	210	150	75

Average Rate of Return

$$\text{Average net income} = \frac{\text{Total net income}}{\text{Investment life}}$$

$$= \frac{325,000}{5} = \$65,000/\text{year}$$

$$\text{Average investment} = \frac{\text{Total investment}}{2}$$

$$= \frac{250,000}{2} = \$125,000$$

$$\text{ARR} = \frac{\text{Average net income}}{\text{Average investment}} = \frac{65,000}{125,000} = 52.0\%$$

Payback

Payback period is 2.52 years. After two years, $140,000 has been recovered from the $250,000 investment. The remaining $110,000 is collected about halfway through year three ($\frac{110,000}{210,000} = .52$).

Present Value

At the required annual ROI of 20 percent, the total present value of the investment is $326,000, much greater than the $250,000 cost of the investment. The net present value is $76,000 and the profitability index is 1.30.

Present Value Calculation

Year	1	2	3	4	5
Cash flow (000)	$40	$100	$210	$150	$75
Discount factor (20%)	.83	.69	.58	.48	.40
Present value (000)	32.2	69	121.8	72	30
Total present value:	$326,000				

Net present value = 326,000 − 250,000 = $76,000

Profitability index = $\frac{326,000}{250,000}$ = 1.30

Internal Rate of Return

Using a return on investment of 32 percent, total present value is $248,100, just less than the $250,000 investment cost. Thus, the IRR is about 32 percent.

Year	Cash Flow ($000)	IRR @ 20% Discount Factor	IRR @ 20% Present Value	IRR @ 32% Discount Factor	IRR @ 32% Present Value
1	40	.83	33.2	.76	30.4
2	100	.69	69.0	.57	57.0
3	210	.58	121.8	.44	92.4
4	150	.48	72.0	.33	49.5
5	75	.40	30.0	.25	18.8
Total present value ($000)			326.0		248.1
− Investment cost ($000)			248.1		248.1
Net present value ($000)			77.9		0

## PART SIX

Managing the Cost of Funds

This part includes the following chapters:

The company has a variety of financial sources, each with its particular characteristics as to cost and terms. These financing alternatives must be identified and evaluated in order to determine the lowest-cost mix of financing possible consistent with preserving the necessary financial flexibility.

Short-Term Financing

Short-term funds are supplied by many sources. Non–interest-bearing financing is supplied by those who allow the company to "pay on time.'' The primary example of non–interest-bearing financing is trade creditors (accounts payable). Trade creditors allow customers (e.g. other companies) to pay on time. Although such sources do not require payment of interest, they can have significant *hidden* costs.

Long-Term Financing

A company's long-term financing is called its capital structure. There are three basic types of capital funds available to a corporation:

- Long-term debt
- Preferred equity
- Common equity

Each of the suppliers of funds to a company expects to realize a return. In the case of lenders, this return is the same thing as the interest rate on new borrowings the company may consider.

Investors who buy the preferred stock of a company also expect to receive a return. This return is in the form of dividends. Preferred stockholders are exposed to greater risk than debt investors, because preferred stockholders cannot receive any dividends until debt investors have received payments due. Thus, preferred stockholders expect greater returns than those received by lenders.

Investors who buy the common stock of a company and who permit their earnings to be reinvested also expect to receive a return. This return is generally in the form of dividends and stock price appreciation. Common stock investors are exposed to the greatest investment risk in a company, since declines in profits and incurrence of losses are absorbed immediately and directly by common stockholders. Thus, common stockholders expect the highest returns of all investors in the company.

Cost of Capital

The cost of capital is the average after-tax return required by all the company's long-term investors. Thus, the cost of capital is the minimum acceptable level of ROI performance which investors expect from you over time. If your ROI is less than the cost of capital, the first group to suffer is the common stockholders. If your ROI is greater than the cost of capital, the common stockholders will gain. The cost of capital is also the minimum acceptable compound ROI that an investment must produce to be acceptable.

## 31

Short-Term Financing

EXECUTIVE SUMMARY

The principal short-term sources of financing for most companies are trade credit and short-term bank loans. When financing needs are great and bank credit is difficult to get, many companies increase their reliance on trade credit. They do this by becoming slow payers, passing up discounts for early payment. This can turn out to be the most expensive form of financing used by the company. Although no interest is explicitly paid on trade credit, missing the discount date can mean an effective interest cost of 40 percent or more.

Since sales can be volatile, working capital and financing requirements can also be volatile. If a company's financing needs are expected to be temporary, short-term debt is usually the most appropriate way to finance. Short-term financing usually accounts for about half of total current assets.

A principal source of short-term financing is known as "spontaneous" financing because it automatically increases with the level of sales and production activities. This spontaneous credit is known as trade credit and is represented by the accounts payable on the balance sheet.

Trade credit is normally available for the financing of some portion of inventory. Other short-term requirements must be met by borrowing from banks or through other financing arrangements.

Trade Credit

Trade credit is activated by simply placing an order with a supplier who allows payment on time. Trade credit terms frequently provide incentives for early payment. For example, terms of "2/10, net 30" mean that you will receive a 2 percent reduction off the invoice if you pay within ten days of the invoice date. Otherwise the entire invoice is due within thirty days of the invoice date.

Cost of Missing Discounts

Although no interest expense is paid on accounts payable financing, it is usually very costly to miss the discount on an invoice whenever allowed. With terms of "2/10, net 30," missing the discount means that it costs you 2 percent of the invoice for the use of trade credit twenty days. This is an effective cost of about 37 percent per year.

Let's say you have an invoice for $100. If you pay the invoice on the tenth day, you would pay $98. If you do not take the discount, then on the thirtieth day you pay $100. In other words, to get use of the $98 for twenty more days, you had to pay a penalty of $2. This penalty amounts to about 2 percent interest for the twenty days; or, 36.7 percent per year. If you can borrow at anything less than 36.7 percent, you will save money by taking the discount.

Let's say you can borrow from the bank at 20 percent per year. On the tenth day you borrow $98 from the bank and take the discount. On the thirtieth you repay the bank $98 plus interest. Interest at 20 percent per year is equivalent to .056 percent per day or 1.1 percent for twenty days. On borrowings of $98 for twenty days, interest will be $1.09. So you will pay the bank $99.09 on the thirtieth day. This is still a savings to you of almost $1 on an invoice of $100.

Taking discounts can save the company a lot of money. It is so important that many companies show "discounts taken" as part of the income on the income statement. It is not rare for discounts taken to represent a material part of total profits.

Discount Formula

The effective cost of missing discounts can be easily calculated with the discount formula:

$$\text{Effective annual interest rate} = \frac{\text{Discount}}{100 - \text{Discount}} \times \frac{360}{\text{Payment period} - \text{Discount period}}$$

At terms of 2/10 net 30, this means:

$$\frac{2}{100 - 2} \times \frac{360}{30 - 10} = 36.7\%$$

Bank Borrowing

Some type of bank borrowing is usually available even to small firms, if they are sound and profitable. An important type of bank borrowing is the line of credit, which the firm can draw against to meet certain types of requirements. Lines of credit are typically considered to be "self-liquidating," since the purpose for which they are extended is expected to provide the means of repayment. For example, if you borrow on a line of credit to finance accounts receivable, as the receivables are collected, you will repay the bank.

With a line of credit, you usually draw down funds as needed. As the funds are repaid, they automatically become available for future borrowing. A line of credit arrangement is similar to a revolving charge account. As you pay down your account, you can continue charging. A line of credit is better than an ordinary bank loan, since with a line of credit you borrow only as much as you need when you need it.

Compensating Balances

In return for providing a line of credit to the company, the bank typically expects compensation in addition to the explicit interest rate charged on borrowings (e.g. prime rate, prime rate plus 2 percent, and so on). Sometimes the added compensation is simply a "commitment fee," which is like a retainer. More commonly, the bank may require compensating balances equal to some fixed percentage of the total line, or the amount being borrowed, or some other basis. Compensating balances are the same thing as average deposit balances in your personal bank account. For example, a compensating balance requirement of 20 percent on a $100,000 line of credit means that, on the average, your bank account must show a daily balance of at least $20,000. That leaves only $80,000 available for use, maximum. As far as the bank is concerned, you are borrowing $100,000, even though you have effective use of only $80,000. This has the result of raising the effective borrowing cost to you.

Assume that you borrow at 18 percent from the bank with a 20 percent compensating balance requirement (based on the total line). The total borrowing is $100,000, of which you have effective use of only $80,000. Interest cost on the total borrowing is $18,000. Your "real" cost of the $80,000 that you have use of is thus,

$$\text{Effective interest rate per annum} = \frac{18,000}{80,000} = .225, \text{ or } 22.5\%$$

A consolation, however, is that the company normally has balances in its checking account which it keeps for operating and safety requirements. The normal (or "working") balances can be used to offset compensating requirements and thus reduce the cost of bank borrowing.

Secured Versus Unsecured Loans

Self-liquidating lines of credit and short-term promissory notes are usually made on the general strength and liquidity of the company over the immediate future. At times, however, even the immediate future may be clouded, and a company may be requesting bank funds for its very survival. In such circumstances the level of risk to the bank is obviously greater and the bank will try to improve the safety of the loan by requiring a pledge of various assets such as accounts receivable or inventory. Securing the bank loan in this manner will give the bank a prior, privileged claim to assets in the event the company should be forced into bankruptcy.

Other Short-Term Sources

There are more specialized sources of financing employed by firms that reflect both the particular strengths and the needs of individual companies and industry practices. Two fairly specialized short-term sources commonly encountered are commercial paper and accounts receivable factoring.

Commercial paper is an important source of financing for large "blue chip" corporations. Commercial paper is sold in the "money market" through middlemen, known as "dealers." Purchasers of commercial paper are typically other large corporations with temporary cash surpluses. Commercial paper is usually issued for six months or less and is often used for temporary financing requirements. There are at least two strong attractions in commercial paper financing: It may be cheaper than bank borrowing, and it decreases reliance on bank sources. I know of one situation, a large utility company, which saved almost $600,000 in one year alone by using commercial paper instead of borrowing from its bank at the prime rate!

In a factoring arrangement, the company sells its receivables to a financial institution known as a factor. The factor takes title to the accounts receivable and, after a specified payment period, allowing time for the collection of receivables by the factor, remits the receivables proceeds (less a discount of 1 to 3 percent and a reserve for disputed items). By assuming the credit functions of the company, the factor relieves the company of these expenses. If the company needs cash before the factor is scheduled to make payment, the company can get an advance against future payments. The advance represents a loan from the factor to the company and interest is charged on the advance. Receivables factoring is commonplace in certain industries, such as the textiles industry. Factoring is also employed by smaller companies that have exhausted other means of financing.

Bank Term Loans

Banks provide a significant portion of term credit. Such loans are rapidly amortized and permit banks to partake of higher-yielding credit investments without exposing the bank to excessive risk or illiquidity.

Beyond loan collateralization and amortization requirements, banks normally specify a number of other conditions the borrower must observe in order to qualify for the loan. Those loan conditions which *prohibit* certain management actions are known as "negative covenants," and those conditions which *require* management to do specific things are known as "positive covenants."

Negative Covenants

Negative covenants include such things as:

1. No dividends above a specified level
2. Restriction on capital expenditures
3. Restrictions on any other debt

Positive Covenants

Positive covenants require certain management actions. Some common positive covenants are:

1. Minimum level of working capital
2. Frequent financial reports
3. Approval from bank for expansion plans

Positive and negative covenants can do much to improve the safety of the bank loan. However, if too stringent, covenants can lead to the opposite effect. For example, if they force a company to forgo certain necessary improvements or to pass up certain important opportunities, impairing the firm's ability to stay competitive and provide the bank safety, such covenants may actually reduce the safety of the loan.

## 32

Long-Term Financing

EXECUTIVE SUMMARY

The long-term financing of a company comprises its capital structure. These are funds provided for a long period of time and therefore subject to considerable risk. There are three basic types of long-term capital:

- Long-term debt
- Preferred stock
- Common stock

Within these generic groups there are special forms. For example, there is secured and unsecured long-term debt; there is convertible debt and convertible preferred stock. Each type of financing used by the company has a unique cost.

The basic objective of capital structure management is twofold:

- Preserve flexibility (always have more than one alternative)
- Minimize the weighted average cost of all funds used

The capital structure of a firm refers to its composition of long-term funds. Since funds in a corporations capital structure are normally varied with respect to type and cost, one can think of the entire right-hand side of a balance sheet as a type of "capital portfolio" in which the long-term funds represent the permanent mix of financing obtained.

Table 32.1 presents a hypothetical capital structure for Ace Corporation. The percentage distribution indicates the relative importance of each financing type as a source of long-term capital.

TABLE 32.1.   Ace Corporation Capitalization

Sources of Financing	Amount ($Mill.)		% of Total Long-Term Capital	
Long-term debt	$15.0		30%	
Preferred stock	2.5		5%	
Shareholders' equity	32.5		65%	
Paid-in capital		5.0		10%
Paid-in surplus		2.5		5%
Retained earnings		25.0		50%
Total long-term capital	$50.0		100%	

At first glance you might wonder why a firm would have more than one type of long-term funds. Why not simply select the lowest-cost source of funds? The answer is that certain mixes of capital with different risk/cost characteristics provide a lower average cost than complete reliance on any single type. As you increase reliance on, for example, bank debt, bankers become anxious about the level of exposure they have in your company, and their required returns will begin to rise higher and higher.

The appearance of each type of security in the firm's capital structure indicates a great deal about its relative standing or importance and, more specifically, about its relationship to either debt or equity-financing. Let us review a capital structure containing the principal long-term debt securities.

Long-Term Debt

Mortgage Debt

Mortgage debt of a firm represents an obligation secured by a particular asset. For example, a firm may wish to buy a particular facility or machine, which it wishes to finance with a mortgage.

Let us assume that you are considering construction of a $1 million facility and approach an insurance company for possible financing. Depending upon the prospects for the company, the use to which the facility will be put, and its expected market value in the event the company should fail and the facility would have to be sold, the insurance company may be willing to lend you some percentage of the cost. If prospects for the company are excellent and the property is likely to keep a high market value, the insurance company may be willing to grant a substantial portion of the cost of the facility. In the event something should happen to the company and it should be forced into liquidation, the insurance company would have exclusive rights to the realizable value of the facility up to its mortgage amount. Thus if the insurance company were to loan you $800,000 against the facility and you were to go bankrupt, the insurance company would immediately seize the facility. If the facility were to be sold for $900,000, the insurance company would receive its $800,000 and the remaining $100,000 would be available to meet claims of other creditors to the corporation and distribution to shareholders of any residual. Mortgage lending is relatively safe to creditors.

Other Secured Debt

Besides a specific mortgage on particular assets, any or all other assets of a corporation may be secured by creditors. Typical secured assets include such things as accounts receivable, inventories, and equipment. Although securing debt increases the relative safety of creditors, they may be reluctant to secure lending too strictly, since it is likely to discourage other financing sources to the company. Within some prudent range, creditors desire participation in the financing of a firm by others, since it may result in more financial flexibility to the firm and thus improve the prospects for successful operations. For example, if a growing company is likely to have expanding capital requirements in support of profitable growth, particular creditors will not want to make it overly difficult for the firm to secure needed financial support from other sources, which will make the growing firm less completely dependent upon one particular creditor.

Unsecured Debt

Unsecured debt is protected by all the unsecured assets of a firm plus what might be available from secured assets after secured creditors are paid off. Thus, if you can conceptualize a "waiting line" among sources of finance to a corporation in which the position in the queue signifies priority of claims to assets in the event of liquidation, unsecured creditors would follow mortgage holders with senior claims upon assets. In the event of liquidation, then, senior creditors would be paid off before junior or subordinated creditors.

Subordinated Creditors

Among straight debt securities, subordinated creditors agree to subordinate their claims. As you would guess, by subordinating their claims such creditors agree to stand farther back in the waiting line and thus incur significant risk. A reasonable question is why a creditor would willingly subordinate his claim to other creditors. The answer is that by incurring the additional risk the subordinated creditor will demand and receive higher returns than other creditors. Even though subordinated creditors have riskier claims relative to all other creditors, they are still protected by other investors even more junior (principally stockholders).

Subordinated Convertible Debt

Subordinated convertible debt is a type of "hybrid" security which combines features of both debt and common stock. As before, the subordinated feature of the security means that the holders of such debt agree to subordinate their claims to all nonsubordinated debt holders. But this security differs from straight subordinated debt because of its convertible feature.

The convertible feature means that the debt can be exchanged on some stipulated basis for common stock of the corporation. For example, a $1000 subordinated convertible bond may be convertible at $20 per share into common stock. On such terms, then, one bond of this debt would be exchangeable into fifty shares of common stock.

Subordinated convertible debt is considered an attractive mix of debt and equity securities for the following reasons. As a "debt" security the security holder receives stipulated, periodic interest income. Moreover, if the company's profitability should increase, as normally expected when such securities are issued, the company's stock price should rise. For example, the stock price might rise to $25 or $30 per share. In such a case the bond holder could convert into common stock at a cost of $20 per share and realize an immediate capital gain of $5 to $10 per share, or $250 to $500 per $1,000 bond.

The possibility of substantial gain on the equity feature of the convertible normally means that the straight interest portion of total return received by such creditors is relatively low. For example, senior debt holders might receive a return of 10 percent on debt, which they get completely from interest payments (having no chance for capital gains). Subordinated convertible debt holders might expect a total return of 15 percent, of which only 7 percent is from interest and the other 8 percent will be expected from capital gains.

The fact that a substantial portion of the return to such creditors will come from expected capital gains can be an important source of risk. For example if capital gains do not materialize such investors will have to be content with a fixed return of 7 percent and debt claims that are subordinated to those of all other creditors.

Preferred Stock

Most preferred stock is cumulative. That is, if a dividend payment is missed it must be made up later. There are other protections to preferred stockholders. For example, if a specified number of dividend payments are missed, management control may be taken from the common shareholders and put into the hands of the preferred shareholders. Moreover, normally, any dividends due to preferred shareholders must be paid before common shareholders can receive any dividends.

Since preferred stock is much like debt, though much more expensive, one might wonder why firms issue it. The answer lies in the safety such financing adds to the capital structure. As an equity buffer, preferred stock makes all types of debt (including subordinated) much more attractive and thus reduces the cost of such financing. Moreover, it is much safer to the corporation in the event the firm should experience reverses. If the firm runs into cash shortage, missing a dividend payment will not force bankruptcy.

Convertible Cumulative Preferred

Convertible cumulative preferred stock is like regular preferred stock except that it can be converted into some specified number of common stock shares the way convertible debt can. For example if a $100 share of convertible preferred can be converted at $20, and the common stock price should rise to $25 or $30 per share, preferred shareholders could exchange a $100 share for five shares of common, on which they could realize a capital gain of $5 to $10 per share.

This type of preferred is obviously attractive, since it combines a fixed periodic income (i.e., the preferred dividend) with some potential for capital gains. Offsetting this, as one might expect, the promised dividend is substantially below that of straight preferred.

Common Stock

Common stock represents the last position in the waiting line in the event the company goes into liquidation. Thus all other security holders must be paid off before common shareholders can receive any of the proceeds of liquidation. As owners of the corporation, the common shareholders possess rights and potential claims to benefits unavailable to any other investors. For example, all profits net of preferred dividends are owned by common shareholders. Thus common shareholders possess the greatest risk and the greatest return of all investors in the corporation.

## 33

Average Cost of Capital

EXECUTIVE SUMMARY

The cost of capital is the composite ROI required by suppliers of long-term funds to the corporation. Since there are tax advantages from using debt financing, the overall ROI standard is calculated on an after-tax basis.

Whenever you fail to earn the cost of capital, it is the stockholders who get shorted. Whenever you outperform the cost of capital, it is the stockholders who get the surplus. The value of the company's common stock is therefore related to its overall ROI performance and future ROI prospects.

The cost of capital is not only the minimum ROI performance standard, it should also be the minimum expected from new investments. If investments are undertaken whose intrinsic compound ROI is below the cost of capital, performance is doomed to be subpar despite the most aggressive attempts at superior managerial performance.

The cost of capital is thus a strategic performance standard. Yet the calculation of the company's cost of capital is extremely difficult to do. The main problem is trying to determine the cost of equity funds used by the company. Several approaches are tried, but ultimately I think the safest thing to do is to get some idea of the range of possible costs and see how investment choices and performance evaluations are affected.

The cost of capital is a crucial concept in investment analysis, because it tells you what the minimum acceptable ROI should be from the investment. If the investment does not provide an ROI at least as great as the cost of capital, it will not be worth undertaking.

The cost of capital, most simply, is the average cost of the funds you need to raise in order to make investments.

Assume that you are considering an investment that requires outlays of $100,000. You plan to raise $50,000 from the owners and $50,000 from long-term debt. The cost of equity is 20 percent after taxes. The cost of debt 8 percent after taxes. Your average cost of capital is then 14 percent after taxes.

$$\text{Average cost of capital} = .5\ (8\%) + .5\ (20\%)$$
$$= 4\% + 10\%$$
$$= 14\% \ (\text{after taxes})$$

Unless the proposed investment offers an ROI of at least 14 percent per year after taxes, over its life, you should reject it.

If the investment will produce exactly 14 percent after taxes, you should accept it, since it will provide owners and lenders the returns they expect. And if the investment will produce more than 14 percent after taxes, you should also undertake the investment, since it will provide shareholders with more than their 20 percent return.

Why a Weighted Average Cost of Capital

Investment funds come from many different sources. Each source of funds has a different cost. Short-term funds have a different cost from long-term funds. The cost of debt is different from the cost of equity.

The weighted average cost of funds is a composite of the different costs of funds used. Each type of funds is weighted by the relative proportion to be used in financing the investment.

Accurate estimates of the costs of capital are difficult at best, and I shall only suggest how each of these is developed.

The Cost of Debt

The pretax cost of debt is reflected in the interest expense you have to pay. However, unlike other types of capital, the cost of debt financing is tax deductible. The tax deductibility of interest expense reduces the effective cost of debt. In figuring the weighted average cost of funds, the after-tax cost of debt should be used.

Consider the two statements below. Number 1 shows net income for a company without any debt. Number 2 shows net income for a company with $100,000 of debt at an interest rate of 10 percent per annum, which requires interest payments of $10,000 per year.

	(Thousands of dollars)	
	# 1	# 2
Sales	$1,000	$1,000
Cost of goods sold	600	600
Gross profit	400	400
Operating expenses	200	200
Interest expense	0	10
Profit before taxes	200	190
Taxes	100	95
Profit after taxes	100	95

In other words, the $10,000 interest expense reduces net income by only $5,000, so the effective cost is only $5,000 on a $100,000 loan, or 5 percent per annum.

The effective (after-tax) cost of debt is equal to the pretax cost times 1 minus the tax rate:

$$\text{After-tax cost of debt} = \text{Pre-tax cost} \times (1 - \text{tax rate})$$
$$= 10\% \times (1-.5)$$
$$= 5\%$$

The Cost of Preferred Stock

The cost of preferred stock funds is easily calculated. You simply divide the preferred stock dividend by the current market price of the preferred stock.

Assume that the dividend on the preferred stock is $8 per share per annum and the current market price of the preferred stock is $50 per share. The cost of preferred stock financing is 16 percent. Since dividends are not a tax-deductible cost to the company, the 16 percent is also the after-tax cost of preferred stock financing.

The Cost of Common Stock

The cost of equity funds is the most difficult to estimate, since there is no contractual obligation in the sense of debt interest expense. This leads some managers to believe incorrectly that internally generated funds are "costless." This is a serious error. The owners bear much greater risks than any other providers of funds to the company. For this reason, the owners expect much greater return on their invested capital than do long-term lenders, for example. If you consistently fail to produce the returns that shareholders require, your value as a manager and the value of the company will decrease. Conversely, if you consistently outperform the expected returns of shareholders, your value as a manager and the value of the company will consistently increase.

Shareholders expect dividends and capital appreciation from their investment in the company. The capital appreciation realized in turn depends on the growth in expected future dividends. Even for companies that pay no dividends, the capital appreciation reflects the increase in expected future dividends. This is obviously hard to estimate, but two popular methods are described below.

For Mature, Dividend-paying Companies:
The Dividend Valuation Model

The dividend valuation model assumes that the cost of equity is reflected in the relationship of stock price to dividends per share. According to this method, shareholders expect returns to be generated by dividends (if any) and increased stock price. The increased stock price, in turn, reflects the expected future growth in dividends per share.

To use this method, compute the ratio of the expected dividend per share during the coming year to the current stock price and add the long-run expected growth rate in dividends (or, as some would prefer, earnings) per share.

Cost of equity = Dividend yield + growth rate

$$= \frac{\text{Dividends per share}}{\text{Stock price}} + \begin{array}{l}\text{Growth rate}\\ \text{expected in dividends}\\ \text{per share}\end{array}$$

Investors expect your company to pay a dividend of $5 per share next year. Dividends have grown at the rate of 7 percent per year, and they are expected to continue growing at this rate. Your stock is selling for $50 per share.

$$\text{Cost of equity} = \frac{\$5}{\$50} + 7\%$$
$$= 17\%$$

Other Methods

When companies don't pay dividends, the dividend valuation method cannot be readily applied. In such cases estimates or approximations on other bases are necessary. Some methods are described below.

Risk Premium Method.   One method for estimating the cost of common equity uses a premium over the pretax cost of debt. The rationale is that equity investors expect a higher return than the company's creditors, because equity investors must bear much more risk. The extra, higher return for assuming the higher risk of stock ownership is known as a risk premium over debt, and this premium is believed to range from 4 percent to 10 percent above the returns to long-term debt investors.

Earnings/Price Method.   A popular, though less reliable, method for estimating the cost of common stock financing is the earnings/price method. This involves taking the ratio of earnings per share to stock prices.

$$\text{Cost of equity} = \frac{\text{Earnings per share}}{\text{Stock price}}$$

Assume that earnings per share are $2.40 and that stock price is $15 per share.

$$\text{Cost of equity} = \frac{\$2.40}{\$15}$$
$$= 16\%$$

Notice that the share price of $15 is exactly 6.25 times the earnings per share of $2.40. In other words, the price/earnings multiple is 6.25 times. The price/earnings multiple is the inverse of the earnings/price ratio.

Book ROE Method

Many firms do not have publicly traded stock and therefore cannot use stock price directly to compute the cost of equity. In such firms the historical return on equity ratio (i.e., net income divided by average shareholders' equity) should provide a reasonable estimate as to what level of return investors are expecting.

Target ROE

Finally, management may decide to set its own target for returns on shareholder investment. If so, this target should be incorporated in the calculation of the cost of capital.

Assume that management decides that shareholders should expect a 30 percent return after taxes on investments. Assume also that the after-tax cost of debt is 5 percent and that investments will be equally financed with debt and equity. In order to meet its targets, management should not accept any investments whose returns are less than 17.5 percent after taxes.

$$\text{Cost of capital} = .5(5\%) + .5(30\%)$$
$$= 2.5\% + 15\%$$
$$= 17.5\%$$

Combining the Costs: The Weighted Average Cost of Capital

To get a weighted average, multiply each cost by its relative proportion in total financing and add up all sources.

Source	Percentage of Total Sources	After-Tax Cost	Weighted Cost
Debt	40%	6%	2.4%
Equity	60%	20%	12.0%
		Total weighted average	14.4%

The weighted average cost of capital for this company is 14.4 percent after taxes.

How to Reduce the Average Cost of Capital

The principal way to decrease the overall cost of capital is to take advantage of the tax shield provided by interest expense. That means using proportionally more debt. However, as the use of debt increases, the riskiness of stock ownership increases (i.e., the financial risk in the company increases), and the returns required on equity will increase.

Cost of Capital: Three Financing Mixes

	A	B	C
After-tax cost of debt	4%	5%	8%
After-tax cost of equity	20%	24%	28%
Proportion of debt used	0	30%	70%
Proportion of equity used	100.0%	70%	30%
Weighted average cost of capital	20%	18.3%	14%

Importance of Minimizing Cost of Capital

By simply reducing your cost of capital you can transform a marginal or even a poor investment into a profitable one. Let's say that you and I manage rival companies and we are both considering an investment in a new consumer product. The product is expected to produce an after-tax return on investment of 15 percent. The investment will cost $100,000. Assume that you have financing mix A and I have financing mix C.

	YOU	ME
EBIT (30% ROI)	30,000	30,000
Debt interest	0	11,200
EBT	30,000	18,800
Taxes (50%)	15,000	9,400
Net income	15,000	9,400
ROE	15,000	9,400
	$\overline{100,000} = 15\%$	$\overline{30,000} = 31\%$

How It Works

	YOU	ME
Total investment	100,000	100,000
Debt financing	0	70,000
Equity financing	100,000	30,000
Financing costs (after taxes)		
Debt financing	NA	8%
Equity financing	20%	28%
Investment ROI		
After-tax	15%	15%

  With the identical investment, your shareholders will get an ROE of only 15 percent, as against compared to the 20 percent they require. My shareholders get 31 percent, above the 28 percent they require!

## 34

Risk-adjusted Cost of Capital

EXECUTIVE SUMMARY

The weighted average cost of capital is the minimum required return from investments of average corporate risk. Investments with greater than average risk, such as new product proposals, should produce above average returns. Investments whose returns can be reliably estimated, such as cost-reduction and replacement projects, may be justified even if they produce returns below the average cost of funds.

The company's overall average cost of capital is a reliable ROI standard for investment proposals similar in risk to those currently undertaken by the company. However, when the risk of a proposed investment is considerably different from those already undertaken, the cost of capital must be adjusted.

The most appropriate way to adjust the cost of capital is to determine what the required rate of return and the financing mix would be for that individual project. But this is usually very difficult, if not impossible, to do.

Risk-adjusted Rates

Large, multidivisional companies whose divisions vary widely in the level of risk frequently establish divisional ROI hurdles rather than individualized project ROI hurdles. The cost of capital for the "riskier" divisions is arbitrarily adjusted above the average cost of capital for the overall firm. The cost of capital for less risky divisions is arbitrarily set below the overall average.

Let's say you work for an oil company. One division is involved in oil exploration, and another division is involved in the operation of an interstate natural gas pipeline. If the overall average cost of capital is 15 percent for the firm, the exploration division might have a cost of capital arbitrarily set at 20 percent, while the pipeline operations have a cost of capital arbitrarily set at 10 percent.

## 35

The Cost of Capital
and Investments

EXECUTIVE SUMMARY

The cost of capital is an ideal investment standard because it clearly defines the minimum returns the investment should produce. The cost of capital is a weighted average composite of required compound rates of return from all long-term suppliers of investment funds. If investment returns exceed the cost of capital, the main beneficiaries are the shareholders. If investment returns just equal the cost of capital, each group of investors gets exactly its required return. If investment returns are below the cost of capital, the shareholders are the primary losers.

In order to see the practical advantages of using the cost of capital in screening investments, consider the following investment, which promises to yield exactly its cost of capital, after taxes.

Investment required: $100,000

Financing:
  Debt $40,000
  Equity $60,000

Cost of funds:
  Debt   12% pre-tax; 6% after-taxes
  Equity 20%

Weighted average
  cost of capital: .4 (6%) + .6 (20%) = 14.4%

Investment
ROI: 14.4% after taxes; 28.8% pretax

Given the above investment information, let's see what the income statement would look like:

Income Statement (abbreviated)

EBIT (28.8%) on investment of $100,000 =	$28,800
Interest (12% on borrowings of $40,000) =	4,800
Pretax income =	24,000
Taxes =	12,000
Net income =	12,000

Shareholders receive $12,000 on an investment of $60,000, for a return of 20 percent after taxes. Lenders receive $4,800 on their investment of $40,000, a return of 12 percent.

If the investment produces anything above 14.4% after taxes, the returns to shareholders will be more than the 20 percent they require and the value of their investment will increase. However, if the after-tax return is below 14.4 percent, the returns to shareholders will be less than the 20 percent they require and the value of their investment will decrease.

Glossary

Accelerated depreciation   A shift in the pattern of asset writeoffs so that greater depreciation is charged off in the early years of an asset's life and less is charged off in the asset's later years. The two methods of accelerated depreciation are (1) double-declining balance method and (2) sum-of-the-years-digits method.

Accrual   A short-term obligation that has been shown as an expense on the income statement but has not been paid. Common accruals are employee wages and tax liabilities.

Aging schedule   A schedule used to determine what percentage of accounts receivable are current and what percentage are overdue. For example, a company might determine that 20 percent of its accounts receivable are "current" (not overdue), 50 percent might be up to thirty days overdue, 20 percent might be from thirty to sixty days overdue, and 10 percent might be more than sixty days overdue.

Bond   A long-term debt security sold by a corporation. Bonds are usually sold in denominations of $1,000.

Book value   (1) An asset's accounting value. Gross book value represents the original (historical) cost of the asset. Net book value is the value of the asset after accumulated depreciation has been subtracted from gross book value.

(2) Book value per share is equal to total shareholders' equity (net worth) divided by the number of common stock shares outstanding.

Break-even analysis   An analysis that shows the relationships among product price-cost-sales variables. Break-even analysis can be used for risk analysis, pricing decisions, production decisions, and financing decisions. It is used to determine the minimum sales level needed to avoid losses.

Capital budgeting   The process for making investment decisions that will last more than a year.

Capital gains (losses)   Profits (or losses) made on the sale of assets. The gains are long-term if the assets have been held for more than a year. The losses are long-term if the assets have been held for more than a year.

Capital markets   Financial markets where long-term (i.e., maturities of more than one year) securities are bought and sold. The New York Stock Exchange is an example of a capital market.

Capital rationing   A situation where acceptable investment opportunities exceed (in total dollars) the amount of money available for investment.

Capital structure   A company's total long-term (or permanent) financing. Capital structure includes financing from long-term debt, preferred stock, and common stock.

Capitalization rate   The discount rate applied to prospective earnings or cash flows from an investment.

Carry-back; carry-forward   Losses experienced by a company can be carried back to offset profits earned in earlier years, thus permitting a refund of taxes previously paid. If previous profits do not offset the loss completely, the remaining loss can then be carried forward as an offset to future profits, thereby reducing future taxes.

Cash budget   A detailed estimate of cash inflows and outflows in order to determine the impacts on the corporate cash balance.

Cost of capital   The minimum return on investment which a company must earn in order to satisfy investors. The cost of capital is the same thing as the weighted average cost of capital.

Compounding   The process of growth through reinvestment of earnings.

Convertible bonds   A special type of long-term debt security that can be exchanged by the investor at par into a specified number of common stock shares of the company. The *conversion ratio* specifies the number of shares one convertible bond can be exchanged for. For example, a conversion ratio of 20 means that one $1,000 (face value) convertible bond can be exchanged for twenty shares of common stock. Sometimes convertible bonds specify a *conversion price* instead of a conversion ratio. The effect is the same, however. In this example, the conversion price would be $50 per share. Thus, a $1,000 par value bond could be exchanged for twenty shares.

Covenants Special agreements and restrictions written into loan contracts. Positive covenants require affirmative actions on the part of the borrower, such as submitting financial statements quarterly to the lender or maintaining some minimal level of net working capital. Negative covenants prohibit the borrower from doing certain things such as paying dividends or borrowing from other sources.

Debenture A form of long-term debt. The term "debenture" is used interchangeably with the term "bond." It is a general obligation in the sense that it is secured ("collateralized") by the general assets of the company rather than a specific piece of property.

Debt ratio An overall measure of the amount of debt used by a corporation. The debt ratio is calculated by dividing total liabilities by the total assets of the company.

Degree of combined leverage A measure of the combined effects of operating leverage and financial leverage. The degree of combined leverage measures the effect of a change in sales on net income and earnings per share. For example, a degree of combined leverage of 3.00 means that for each 1 percent change in sales, net income and earnings per share will change by 3 percent, or three times as much. The degree of combined leverage is affected by the level of sales relative to the company's break-even point. As sales move higher and higher above the break-even point, the degree of combined leverage decreases.

Degree of financial leverage A measure of the magnifying effect of fixed financial costs (e.g., interest expense) on net income and earnings per share. A degree of financial leverage of 2.00, for example, means that for every 1 percent change in operating income, net income and earnings per share will change by 2 percent, in other words, twice the rate. The degree of financial leverage is affected by the level of sales relative to the company's break-even point. As the sales level rises higher and higher above the break-even point, the degree of financial leverage decreases.

Degree of operating leverage A measure of the magnifying effect of fixed operating costs (e.g., depreciation) on operating profit. A degree of operating leverage of 1.50, for example, means that for every 1 percent change in sales, operating income will change by 1.5 percent, or one and a half times as much. The degree of operating leverage is affected by the level of sales relative to the company's break-even point. As sales move higher and higher above the break-even point, the degree of operating leverage decreases.

Discount rate   The rate used in valuing cash flows to be received in the future. The discount rate is designed to tell you the investment value of a future amount of cash, given that you want a specified compound return on investment.

Discounted cash flow techniques   Techniques used in evaluating multiyear capital investments. There are two main discounted cash flow techniques: internal rate of return and net present value. The profitability index is a modification of the net present value technique and represents a ratio of discounted future cash flows to the investment required.

Dividend yield   A ratio of annual cash dividends per share divided by the market price per share of common stock.

Du Pont system   A technique for analyzing the determinants of ROI.

Earnings before interest and taxes (EBIT)   A term used synonymously with "operating income" in this book. It is calculated by deducting operating expenses from gross profit.

Economic order quantity (EOQ)   A mathematical formula that minimizes the total costs of ordering and storing inventory.

Earnings per share (EPS)   A quantity calculated by dividing the earnings available for common stockholders by the number of common stock shares outstanding. The figure tells you how much profit was earned for each share of common stock outstanding during the year.

Equity   The amount of investment in the company provided by stockholders. The investment supplied by preferred shareholders is sometimes combined with the investment provided by common stockholders, but equity is normally understood to be common stock equity only. Equity and "net worth" are used interchangeably. Equity comprises two types of investment by shareholders, common stock and retained earnings.

Factoring   A form of financing with accounts receivable. Many types of factoring arrangements are employed. A common arrangement is for the corporation to borrow against receivables sold to a factor.

Financial leverage   A term referring to the use of debt financing by a company. There are many ways to measure the financial leverage employed by a company, the debt ratio being the most comprehensive measure.

Financial markets   Places where financial securities are bought and sold. The principal financial market in the United States is in New York City.

Financial risk   The risk incurred by a company whenever it borrows money. There are two types of financial risk: (1) the risk of defaulting on terms in the loan contract and being forced into bankruptcy and (2) the risk resulting from the degree of financial leverage which has the effect of making net income and earnings per share more volatile.

Financial structure The aspect of a corporation that reflects the way in which assets are being financed. The company's financial structure includes its current liabilities, long-term liabilities, and equity.

Float The delay time between the writing of a check against the bank account and the actual payment of the check by the bank. Mail times are a major source of float. For example, if you write a check on Monday and it is cleared against your account on Friday, float is the time from Monday to Friday.

Goodwill An intangible asset. Goodwill reflects the difference between what has been paid for an asset and its book value. For example, if you pay $100,000 for an asset that has a book value of $60,000, goodwill will be shown as $40,000.

Incremental cash flow The *net* increase in cash flows resulting from an investment decision. For example, if you replace an investment that produces cash flow of $100,000 per year with an investment that produces cash flow of $150,000 per year, the incremental cash flow is $50,000. Of course, incremental cash flows should be compared with the incremental investment involved.

Internal financing The amount of investible funds generated in the normal operations of the company. Internal funds normally equal net income plus depreciation.

Investment tax credit A rebate given by the Federal government on the purchase prices of long-lived assets. For example, if the investment tax credit is 10 percent, you will get $10,000 in tax refunds from the government for an investment of $100,000. Obviously, the investment tax credit is intended as an incentive to make long-term investments.

Line of credit A specified amount of borrowing available to a corporation from a financial institution (usually a bank). The line is available for a specified period of time and can be drawn down as needed. A revolving line of credit is like a charge account, because as it is repaid, the borrowing is automatically made available again.

Liquidity The ability of a company to meet short-term obligations. There are many ways to measure liquidity. For example, the "quick ratio" measures the amount of cash, marketable securities, and accounts receivable relative to total current liabilities.

Lock-box technique A method for accelerating the collection of cash. In this method, customers send payments to a post office box which is monitored by a bank. Several times a day a bank messenger collects all lock-box receipts and the checks are immediately put into the bank check-clearance system. The supporting documents are sent to the company.

Money market   A financial market where short-term securities (maturities of one year or less) are bought and sold.

Mortgage   A type of long-term debt secured ("collateralized") by a specific asset. For example, a company may mortgage its factory building. If the company defaults on its loan contract, the lender (mortgagor) can immediately take possession of the building and has the right to sell the building in order to recover the amount of the loan outstanding.

Operating leverage   The volatility of operating income resulting from the use of fixed operating expenses (e.g. depreciation, rent).

Ordinary income   The profit earned by a company in the normal course of business (e.g. sales minus expenses). Ordinary income is different from capital gains and is taxed at a much higher rate.

Payback period   The length of time before a company recovers its total outlays for an investment. For example, a payback period of three years means that the investment will take three years to generate enough cash flows to recover the investment required.

Net present value   A discounted cash flow technique used in capital budgeting decisions. Net present value compares the time-adjusted value of an investment's future cash flows with the total cost of the investment. If the investment's net present value is zero or better, the investment is worth undertaking. Otherwise the investment should be rejected.

Net worth   A sum calculated by subtracting a company's total liabilities from its total assets. For example, if a company has total assets of $1,000,000 and total liabilities of $300,000, its net worth is $700,000. Since the net worth belongs to shareholders, "net worth" is used interchangeably with "shareholders equity."

Payout ratio   The percentage of earnings that is paid out as dividends to stockholders. The payout ratio is calculated by dividing dividends paid by net income. For example, if a company earns $100,000 and pays out dividends of $60,000, its payout ratio is 60 percent.

Price/earnings (P/E) multiple   A figure that reflects the relative attractiveness of a company's stock among investors. The price/earnings multiple is calculated by dividing the stock price by earnings per share. For example, a company with earnings per share of $1.00 and a market price per share of $10.00 has a P/E of 10 times.

Prime rate   The lowest rate of interest a bank charges borrowers. The prime rate is usually given only to the most creditworthy borrowers.

Pro forma statements   Hypothetical or projected statements that try to show what the effects of a particular decision or course of action will be on the company's financial statements. Pro forma statements are essential for major investment decisions and financing plans.

Profit center   A type of responsibility center in which the responsible manager is evaluated on the basis of profits generated. Since the profit center does not incorporate the amount of investment required to generate profits, it is not as effective a standard as ROI.

Profitability index   A relative measure of an investment's worth. It is calculated by taking a ratio of the present value of a company's future cash flows to the cost of the investment. The higher the profitability index, the more attractive the investment is considered to be.

Reinvestment rate   The amount of ROI which can be earned on cash that is produced by an investment.

Required rate of return   The minimum ROI that must be produced by an investment in order for the investment to be acceptable. The required rate of return is the same thing as the cost of capital for an investment.

Retained earnings   A part of shareholders' equity. Retained earnings are the profits earned by the company that are reinvested in the company. Retained earnings for a given year are equal to net income less dividends paid out.

Risk-adjusted discount rate   A discount rate that reflects the relative amount of risk in an investment under consideration.

Salvage value   The market value of an investment remaining at the end of the investment's life.

Subordinated debenture   A type of long-term debt in which lenders agree to subordinate their claims on assets to other lenders in the event of bankruptcy.

Trade credit   The financing provided by suppliers. Trade credit is usually the same thing as accounts payable.

Weighted average cost of capital   A figure calculated by weighting the cost of each type of financing by its relative proportion in the capital structure of the company.

Yield   The same thing as the overall compound ROI on an investment. Yield is also the same as the internal rate of return on an investment.

Table of ROI Discount Factors

# of years	1%	2%	4%	6%	8%	10%	12%	14%	15%	16%	18%	20%	22%	24%	25%	26%	28%	30%	35%	40%	45%	50%
1	0.990	0.980	0.962	0.943	0.926	0.909	0.893	0.877	0.870	0.862	0.847	0.833	0.820	0.806	0.800	0.794	0.781	0.769	0.741	0.714	0.690	0.667
2	0.980	0.961	0.925	0.890	0.857	0.826	0.797	0.769	0.756	0.743	0.718	0.694	0.672	0.650	0.640	0.630	0.610	0.592	0.549	0.510	0.476	0.444
3	0.971	0.942	0.889	0.840	0.794	0.751	0.712	0.675	0.658	0.641	0.609	0.579	0.551	0.524	0.512	0.500	0.477	0.455	0.406	0.364	0.328	0.296
4	0.961	0.924	0.855	0.792	0.735	0.683	0.636	0.592	0.572	0.552	0.516	0.482	0.451	0.423	0.410	0.397	0.373	0.350	0.301	0.260	0.226	0.198
5	0.951	0.906	0.822	0.747	0.681	0.621	0.567	0.519	0.497	0.476	0.437	0.402	0.370	0.341	0.328	0.315	0.291	0.269	0.223	0.186	0.156	0.132
6	0.942	0.888	0.790	0.705	0.630	0.564	0.507	0.456	0.432	0.410	0.370	0.335	0.303	0.275	0.262	0.250	0.227	0.207	0.165	0.133	0.108	0.088
7	0.933	0.871	0.760	0.665	0.583	0.513	0.452	0.400	0.376	0.354	0.314	0.279	0.249	0.222	0.210	0.198	0.178	0.159	0.122	0.095	0.074	0.059
8	0.923	0.853	0.731	0.627	0.540	0.467	0.404	0.351	0.327	0.305	0.266	0.233	0.204	0.179	0.168	0.157	0.139	0.123	0.091	0.068	0.051	0.039
9	0.914	0.837	0.703	0.592	0.500	0.424	0.361	0.308	0.284	0.263	0.225	0.194	0.167	0.144	0.134	0.125	0.108	0.094	0.067	0.048	0.035	0.026
10	0.905	0.820	0.676	0.558	0.463	0.386	0.322	0.270	0.247	0.227	0.191	0.162	0.137	0.116	0.107	0.099	0.085	0.073	0.050	0.035	0.024	0.017
11	0.896	0.804	0.650	0.527	0.429	0.350	0.287	0.237	0.215	0.195	0.162	0.135	0.112	0.094	0.086	0.079	0.066	0.056	0.037	0.025	0.017	0.012
12	0.887	0.788	0.625	0.497	0.397	0.319	0.257	0.208	0.187	0.168	0.137	0.112	0.092	0.076	0.069	0.062	0.052	0.043	0.027	0.018	0.012	0.008
13	0.879	0.773	0.601	0.469	0.368	0.290	0.229	0.182	0.163	0.145	0.116	0.093	0.075	0.061	0.055	0.050	0.040	0.033	0.020	0.013	0.008	0.005
14	0.870	0.758	0.577	0.442	0.340	0.263	0.205	0.160	0.141	0.125	0.099	0.078	0.062	0.049	0.044	0.039	0.032	0.025	0.015	0.009	0.006	0.003
15	0.861	0.743	0.555	0.417	0.315	0.239	0.183	0.140	0.123	0.108	0.084	0.065	0.051	0.040	0.035	0.031	0.025	0.020	0.011	0.006	0.004	0.002
16	0.853	0.728	0.534	0.394	0.292	0.218	0.163	0.123	0.107	0.093	0.071	0.054	0.042	0.032	0.028	0.025	0.019	0.015	0.008	0.005	0.003	0.002
17	0.844	0.714	0.513	0.371	0.270	0.198	0.146	0.108	0.093	0.080	0.060	0.045	0.034	0.026	0.023	0.020	0.015	0.012	0.006	0.003	0.002	0.001
18	0.836	0.700	0.494	0.350	0.250	0.180	0.130	0.095	0.081	0.069	0.051	0.038	0.028	0.021	0.018	0.016	0.012	0.009	0.005	0.002	0.001	0.001
19	0.828	0.686	0.475	0.331	0.232	0.164	0.116	0.083	0.070	0.060	0.043	0.031	0.023	0.017	0.014	0.012	0.009	0.007	0.003	0.002	0.001	
20	0.820	0.673	0.456	0.312	0.215	0.149	0.104	0.073	0.061	0.051	0.037	0.026	0.019	0.014	0.012	0.010	0.007	0.005	0.002	0.001		
21	0.811	0.660	0.439	0.294	0.199	0.135	0.093	0.064	0.053	0.044	0.031	0.022	0.015	0.011	0.009	0.008	0.006	0.004	0.002	0.001		
22	0.803	0.647	0.422	0.278	0.184	0.123	0.083	0.056	0.046	0.038	0.026	0.018	0.013	0.009	0.007	0.006	0.004	0.003	0.001	0.001		
23	0.795	0.634	0.406	0.262	0.170	0.112	0.074	0.049	0.040	0.033	0.022	0.015	0.010	0.007	0.006	0.005	0.003	0.002	0.001			
24	0.788	0.622	0.390	0.247	0.158	0.102	0.066	0.043	0.035	0.028	0.019	0.013	0.008	0.006	0.005	0.004	0.003	0.002	0.001			
25	0.780	0.610	0.375	0.233	0.146	0.092	0.059	0.038	0.030	0.024	0.016	0.010	0.007	0.005	0.004	0.003	0.002	0.001	0.001			
26	0.772	0.598	0.361	0.220	0.135	0.084	0.053	0.033	0.026	0.021	0.014	0.009	0.006	0.004	0.003	0.002	0.002	0.001				
27	0.764	0.586	0.347	0.207	0.125	0.076	0.047	0.029	0.023	0.018	0.011	0.007	0.005	0.003	0.002	0.002	0.001	0.001				
28	0.757	0.574	0.333	0.196	0.116	0.069	0.042	0.026	0.020	0.016	0.010	0.006	0.004	0.002	0.002	0.001	0.001	0.001				
29	0.749	0.563	0.321	0.185	0.107	0.063	0.037	0.022	0.017	0.014	0.008	0.005	0.003	0.002	0.002	0.001	0.001	0.001				
30	0.742	0.552	0.308	0.174	0.099	0.057	0.033	0.020	0.015	0.012	0.007	0.004	0.003	0.002	0.001	0.001	0.001	0.001				
40	0.672	0.453	0.208	0.097	0.046	0.022	0.011	0.005	0.004	0.003	0.001	0.001										
50	0.608	0.372	0.141	0.054	0.021	0.009	0.003	0.001	0.001	0.001												

Index

Index